ADDICTED TO STRUGGLE

How To Stop Winning This Losing Game

EVAN MARCUS

PUBLISHED BY

PRINTED IN THE US. PUBLISHED AUGUST 2018.

Dedication

This book is dedicated to Love.

"We are going to love you until you learn how to love yourself."

Anonymous

ADDICTED TO STRUGGLE

Table of Contents

Acknowledgements

My friendmentor, Bob Megill, is the first person who used the phrase 'Addicted to Struggle' to describe patterns in my life. He doesn't recall where he first heard the phrase. As soon as I heard it, it stuck. I knew it was a right fit for me. Bob, as a friend and mentor, has been a right fit too. Not only does he help me identify my addiction to struggle, he truly cares about me and wants me to find more freedom and joy.

My friendmentorfatherfigureteacher, Ralph Green, has been on this journey with me for almost 20 years. Like Bob, he too wants me to be happy, joyous, and free in life. Words will never describe the depth and breadth of our relationship. Ralph literally has saved my life; the breathing kind of life and an even bigger kind of life— the being alive life. Everyone should be so blessed to have a Ralph. He truly loves me, and I love him.

There are many folks and friends who help me every day. Through the open sharing of our pain, our dreams, and our lives, we help each other find freedom from addiction and the freedom to live. So much of the words and ideas in this book come from our fellowship.

Let's go right to the source. I am grateful to have a relationship with GodcreatorsourcespirithigherpowerLouie. I know that it's this love that truly is my source of life, of healing, and of this book.

Friendmentor, Stanley Crawford, has helped me find an eclectic experience of the divine. We have many conversations that enlighten me and bring me closer to the Creator. Stanley has helped me realize that everything in my life, including the words, meaning, and impact of this book come through me, from the source of life itself.

My teacher at Antioch University, Don Hanlon Johnson, who many years ago opened my mind and heart to writing. I'm still not sure how he did it, but through Don I learned how to allow creative expression to come through me. I also thank Thommy Barton and Judy Bell who gave me a taste of freedom.

My friends, I can't live well without our conversations, support and love for one another. There is no book, let alone much of a good life, without our friendship.

Donald Seymour has been an important source of encouragement. Our conversations helped me get unstuck and get unleashed at each new step.

Tom Leahy and Bob Minnick, our many conversations keep me alive. One day at a time I unstruggle with your love.

Jim Tretick took 100,000+ words and put them in a form so that I could work with them. He was pure encouragement at a time when I needed it.

Hedy Sirico brings all our work to life; her design work is indispensable. She is incredibly patient with us. We created a verb in her honor. To 'Hedify.'

Our sons Dylan, Daniel, and Andrew inspire and teach me. You each have ways-of-being that are more evolved than me and daily give me guidance on how to live a better life and become a better version of myself. I am so grateful for our family life—its where I feel most at home. I am so grateful that I get to be in life with you.

My loverbestfriendpartnerwife, Tara Marcus, really believed in this message and in me. Her excitement helped encourage me to keep writing and trust the brilliance that was showing up on these pages. Tara's support of my creative endeavors means so much to me and helps fuel my creative expression. *Addicted to Struggle* would not exist without her; neither would our wonderful business nor the wonderful life we are living.

Introduction

I was getting ready to edit the book one more time—to get the grammar right, spelling and punctuation correct, and tighten up the sentences.

"Oh shit, this is going to be a lot of work." Is the voice I heard within me.

Then another voice started to speak to me. "It would be really silly for me to struggle while writing a book about letting go of struggle."

I'd often heard these two voices while writing this book. Each time I heard them, I would wrestle a bit and eventually let go of the struggle. I'd ask myself, "What would help me let go of the struggle right now?"

One voice that came to me was particularly liberating. This voice said, "Write the book for yourself." Writing for myself, without need for other's approval, took away much of my *not good enough* feeling.

When it came to the final edit I felt stuck again. "I just invested 5 years, why not make it right." Thankfully, my unstruggle voice came to my rescue.

"Evan, this book is not like anything else you have written. Let it be the way it is. Trust what has come through you and how it has come through you. The book is done, let it go."

This voice was closer to my voice. I love my writing when it's still a bit raw; I love it imperfect. I like reading it that way. It touches me more. There is room to play with it, engage with it, learn from it.

You will find some spelling mistakes, grammar mistakes, unpolished languaging. I love it this way. I hope you do too.

Something bigger hit me. I know that perfectionism is a key driver of struggle. The need to get things really right, all buttoned up, no errors, is a ripe breeding ground for struggle.

I need to let that go. The messages in this book are strong; stronger than the errors. It gives me freedom to let go of needing it to be perfect.

I trust that voice that told me "it's done—let it go as it is." That should probably be a mantra for my life: "Evan, you are ok just the way you are; you are ok just the way you are; let go and live your life."

I have written two other books. Neither of them has sold a lot or touched that many people. I would like this book to sell a lot of copies and reach a whole slew of people. My unstruggle voice helped here too. "Evan if you want a different result, do something different—Let the book go as it is. See what happens."

When Jim Tretick did the first edit, he broke the book up into bite size chunks to make it easier to edit. He numbered each one. Chapter 1 was filled with 1.1, 1.2, 1.3 etc. Chapter 2 became 2.1, 2.2 etc. I loved it and kept it that way. Each 'psalm' is numbered and has its own title. Each one is its own piece and they also tie into each other. The chunking of the book also took away a lot of struggle for me and made the process easier and clearer. I hope you agree. Another unstruggle strategy that works for me. When I break things down into bite-sized chunks, things go so much easier and are more enjoyable for me; be it the dishes, writing a book, or living one day at a time. Thank you, Jim!

I truly hope the writing style for **Addicted to Struggle** works for you.

In the early 80s I was introduced to something I had been born with but was losing the ability to do—*Play*.

For 30 years I have been enthralled by the possibility of living a play-filled life. I write about it. I experiment with it. I play with it. I discovered that play is a very powerful way to live. But there was a problem. Another very powerful force was inhibiting me from playing and living a happy life—Struggle.

I wanted to write a book about play, but every time I sat down and wrote, what came through me was **Addicted to Struggle**. I fought it; trying to push the wave of struggle away. I felt distracted from my 'real' purpose.

"Will I ever get to finally write all that I know about play?"

"Maybe I'm afraid. It's easier to 'want' to write the book on play than 'to' write the book."

"What if I can't actually write all I know about play?" "Better not to try."

As I tried to write about play, the repetitive waves of struggle kept coming. I finally gave in. The book I was meant to write at this time is **Addicted to Struggle**.

While I didn't write the book on play, the writing of **Addicted to Struggle** helped me to become much freer. I kept making a commitment to let go of my struggle as I wrote. I took on more playful attitudes as I wrote. It just seemed so silly to be *in* struggle while writing a book *about* letting go of struggle. I truly hope that this book helps you, as it has me, find more freedom from your patterns of struggle and more playfulness in your life.

Here's what I realized. Until I find freedom from my patterns of struggle I'll never be able to have the freedom to play.

God bless!

1

Addicted to Struggle

1.1 Addicted to Struggle

We are addicted to struggle and it's killing us. Literally!

We struggle at work, we struggle at home; we struggle with our kids, our weight, our health and our homework. We struggle at everything we do. Do you know why you struggle? It's really important to figure it out. Here's why I struggle—to feel worthy. At the core I don't feel good enough. It's that simple. Not a good enough parent, not a good enough husband, not a good enough leader of executive retreats. When I work out, I don't do a good enough job, I don't eat well enough. When I give a talk, it's not enough. It has nothing to do with how much applause, complements or money I receive. My motor is running on "Evan, I'm not good enough." But I have developed a powerful solution. If I struggle with what I am doing, then I can get enough points to earn my *good enough* merit badge. As long as it's hard, then I can feel like I did something worthwhile. Be it work, cleaning the house, writing a book, or playing with my kids. But there's a big problem with this strategy. It doesn't matter how much I struggle or how hard I work, it doesn't seem to make any real dents in my *not good enough* armor. I do get some kind of weird reward for feeling tired, worn out, or drained. I can look back and tell myself, "wow, look how hard you worked on that." It may give me a short moment of satisfaction, but it doesn't make an impact on the real issue; the underlying feeling or belief that 'I'm not good enough.'

It's an insidious dis-ease, because most of the time we don't even realize what is really going on. We rarely, if ever, hear the words, "I'm not good enough" ringing throughout our bodies. The message is almost never that direct. What we do experience are the symptoms of this disease. We feel bored, or alone, or downright pissed off. We feel afraid; we feel the pains of arthritis, migraine headaches, back pain, and many of the more devastating diseases. We experience the painfulness of chemotherapy, of years of therapy, panic disorders, anxiety, and self-doubt. We feel the shame of looking in the mirror and telling ourselves that we are too fat. We feel the low self-esteem that comes with not being able to keep up a diet, an exercise regimen, or our patience. We suffer from a lack of intimacy with our friends, children, and even our spouses. The symptoms are barking loud and clear all the time but we are not hearing them for who they are. We misinterpret their cry. You may ask yourself. Why would I do that? Why wouldn't I listen? Here's why. It's quite simple. See, if we listened to ourselves and made the changes, we would stop struggling. Sounds pretty good; right? Wrong! See the reason we struggle is to solve our *not good enough* problem. If we stop struggling then we have to deal with the real issue, and that is very scary—Even terrifying. What if I find out that I really am not good enough? That my friends would be one very big problem.

1.2 Divine Love

I often meditate in bed, as I wake up. I enjoy laying there curled up in my blanket. There is no need to sit up, cross my legs, or touch my fingertips. A friend of mine named Kenny; he has passed away, used to tell this story. One day he was sitting in his living room watching an old movie. Something in the movie triggered something deep inside of him. He felt that amazing feeling when the spirit comes to you. Well Kenny got the spirit and not knowing any better he thought he should run upstairs, go to his bedroom, get on his knees alongside his bed and pray. To this point in his life, that was his notion of prayer. So, he leaves the living room and runs up to his bedroom. By the time he got to his bed; the feeling was gone. His lesson; take it where you can get it.

That morning, I woke up and got right into my meditation. It doesn't always connect, but this morning the connection was strong. When it's strong for me, the feeling is very gentle, quiet, and at the same time grounded, firm, and broad. As I started to talk to God, he reminded me of a story my new friend Rick McKnight had told me the previous morning over coffee, about his dad Bill.

In his early 20s, Rick wrote a letter home to his dad, questioning if his dad loved him. His dad lived in Montana, about 600 miles away from Rick in Seattle. It was 6 am; three days after Rick took the courageous act of writing his dad. There was a knock at the door. His dad, the Marlboro man as Rick describes him, was standing there. He had gotten the letter and drove 600 miles to assure his son that he love him. I was blown away by this story. As I laid there meditating, I got in a conversation with God. I was asking for reassurance. And then, spirit blew me away, as poppa Bill blew away Rick.

GodSpirit said to me, "If Bill McKnight was willing to drive 600 miles to reassure his son, how far do you think I am willing to go to reassure you?"

I'm not sure I can describe the feeling that came over me.

As I told Tara the story later that day, I started to cry.

If a human can do this act of love for his son, imagine what a divine force could do with divine love. If there are 7 billion people on the planet, not counting all the animals, plants, bugs, microorganisms, and every other living entity, imagine what it takes for this God, divine power, to be able to pay personal attention to each one of us, as I experienced this morning.

On two occasions in my life, I have called out in frustration. "What am I going to do?" This was not a casual statement. It was one of those raw, frustrated, desperate calls. "What am I going to do?" I wasn't expecting an answer. I wasn't talking to anyone. Sheer life frustration. A bottom.

Twice a voice has answered me directly. Answered me directly. The divine voice, God, Higher Self, whatever you call it, was paying attention to me. I was being watched and cared for. I was being loved by the same force that creates and created universe.

This book isn't about struggle, it's about love.

The antidote for not feeling good enough is not less struggle, it's not more play; it's not doing less, doing more.

The answer for me is simple.

Knowing that I am loved.

No amount of hard work, struggle, or accomplishment will do the trick.

Without knowing we are loved, we will never find the peace, the freedom and happiness that many of us seek. We will never really feel love from others.

Once we begin to seek, discover, and experience this love, then we free ourselves to start playing more, living more, loving more, and letting go of struggle. In this process, we will know freedom, we will experience joy; and we will have a sense of confidence, trust, and accomplishment. We will experience and cultivate ease, our gifts, and grace. Less and less will we need to sabotage, get sick, upset relationships, and lose what we have gained.

We will be more able to enjoy our lives and contribute more whole heartedly to life and to others.

Finding out we are enough and that we are loved is not the end. It's a beginning.

I wonder if the real game is learning how to love ourselves.

1.3 Prologue

My colleague Karen Warner and I were having lunch. Karen is a big fan of our first book *It's O.K. to Play*. She is also a fan of our daily *Games for The Day*. She suggested that I write a prologue to our play book. If I could make the case for 'play' first, then she thought the play concepts would make more accessible to many more people. She thought that senior executives would understand our play concepts if I made that case first. She'd buy a bunch of the books and give them to the senior folks she coaches. The idea of senior execs getting excited about play was exciting to me. My goal is to transform the way we work and live; to create 'play' cultures in all areas of our lives so that our lives are more meaningful; and that we are more engaged, enlivened, and effective in everything we do. As we come to understand the underlying dynamics of playfulness, we see that play is a powerful strategy for living and working, for accomplishing our goals, for being really productive, happy, and joyous. Who doesn't want to be happy and joyous and as successful as possible? I honestly believe that play provides us with a path to accomplishing these lofty goals.

The problem is the assumptions many of us have about the word 'play.' When I talk about play, typically we think of a 'recess' kind of thing, or bouncy balls and toys. We assume that play means: getting away from our serious activities; a break from the real stuff; frivolity. Often play connotes a waste of time. As I've come to understand play, it is quite the opposite. Play is sacred; it's our highest form of living. Play is about focus, unleashing our fullest potential.

It's aliveness, adaptability, vulnerability, accomplishment, collaboration at its finest; usefulness, sustainably, dynamic use of resources. If you continue to read this book, you will come away with a greater appreciation for play. Hopefully you will feel unleashed as I did when I was introduced to the play in its full form. It has been an awesome awakening for me.

For the past 30 years I have been a student of play in my own life, in my work and in my work with others. I truly hope that this book will do for you what 'play' has done for me. Like many aspects in my life, play too is a journey. I am much more playful then I was, and I am still far from being the playmate that I strive to be. I need to read, understand, study and incorporate the concepts in this book as much as anyone.

Addicted to Struggle starts off with an exploration of why and how we create struggle in our lives. This is important because our addiction to struggle trips up our ability to play. As you will find out, our addiction to struggle is a game too, but surely not the game I aspire to play; not the one we were put here to play. The next part of the book goes into finding a solution for our struggle; learning how to un-struggle. This is where play comes into the picture. Play is both a strategy to free us from struggle and an outcome of un-struggling ourselves. For me, to play is to be spiritual. They may be one and the same. Finding the solution to our struggle problem is discovering that we are enough. Beyond enough, we find out that we are truly loved and eventually we may find out that we love ourselves. I am suggesting that our path to finding our *enoughness*, to finding our love, is actually a spiritual journey in itself.

When Karen first suggested I write this book, my first thought (after the excitement of getting the play message to senior execs) was "no f-ing way. I am not going to write this. Too hard. Too much work. The voices in my head tell me that I'm not a writer. I have old voices telling me that, "I'm not smart, certainly not smart enough to write a book. I certainly understand play, but trying to explain it will be too much work for me. I won't do it well enough. Why try.

It will come out weak. I certainly won't look like the play expert I think I am. Better not to try." So, I shut the idea down in my mind and continued through our lunch. After lunch I drove back to my home and office. It's now about 90 minutes after Karen's suggestion and my "no f-ing' way."

Karen's husband was the editor of the Harvard Business Review. He also has written over a dozen books. In my mind this gave Karen's comments some credence. She laid it out so simply to me. "Evan, 10 chapters, 180 pages. No problem." Sounded simple enough, but not the game I wanted to play. Too formulaic for me.

In graduate school at Antioch University in San Francisco I was blessed to work with Don Johnson; the main professor in my study of Somatic Psychology. I thank Don for teaching me how to write. I'm not sure how he taught me. We didn't talk sentence structure, grammar, or outlines. We never even talked explicitly about how to write. Don showed me a new way of learning and engaging with information. He had this idea of seed genius. That within the folks we studied, there were seed geniuses to their ideas. Our work was to find the seed genius and then run it through our own experience, our own thinking, our own lives. Instead of regurgitating ideas, we would create new ones. The underlying thread to our work was to create our own somatic theory influenced by the seed genius of the folks we studied, and each other. In undergraduate school I had trouble writing a 500-word essay. Two pages. The outlines, the opening, the formula, the marks off for wrong grammar. This was before word processing. When we typed the paper, I was so concerned with mistakes that would take points off my grade that I couldn't write. I was trying to follow the formula. I translated this into the idea, "I'm not a good writer." So, imagine how I feel sitting down to write this thesis based on my somatic theory. I had no outline, no preconceived well thought out idea, no real plan—the things I thought real writers had to know before they wrote. To this day I don't know if it was Don's suggestion or it came to me out of the blue. I just started writing. Pencil on paper. A guy who could not write 2 pages, ripped out 50 pages. Unbelievable. The ideas flowed out and through me. In my mind I judged it. "It can't be any good. It won't make sense. How can there be any order? Where are my foot notes?" I was amazed. There was an order. Really good stuff came out. Things I had never really thought of before, certainly not in a systematic way. But I did it, I wrote about my somatic theory. I really loved it.

By the time I got home from lunch with Karen, something within me shifted. I sat down at my desk and started to write. The idea of 'addicted to struggle' was not on my mind. I was surprised to see it come forth. The whole time I was writing this book, it seemed to have nothing to do about play. I can recall telling myself, "Ok, this isn't' the book Karen talked about. I guess I'll have to write that another time." I felt a bit like I was avoiding the real subject. But clearly this is the book, the words, and ideas coming through me. As I did back at Antioch, I sat down to write. Often, I have no idea what I'm going to write. Sometimes I have a question in my mind, one I don't know the answer to until I start writing. I feel like a reader who is watching the words flow out of me. Often, I'm saying to myself, "Wow what a cool idea." Sometimes I wonder; "Does any of this makes sense? Where is this going?" Typically, I write for 10 or 15 minutes at a sprint. Most of my writing sessions go 950 to 1500 words. On a few days, I get on a roll and 4000 words flow out of me.

The one piece I question is the opening. As I sat down to write for the first time, I actually did have a model in my head—The book Good to Great by Jim Collins. Jim lays out the whole book in the first paragraph. Actually, the first sentence. I thought, 'Boy would I love to write a book like that.' I love books that are so clear that the author can do that. Plus, the book was a big hit. I told myself; maybe I want to write like Jim Collins. I sat down and channeled Jim Collins and out came the phrase, 'We are addicted to struggle.' To this day, I'm not sure how authentic it is. It sounds powerful. I think I actually believe it. So please know that the first page feels a bit not like me. The rest came flowing out in the spirit unleashed back in San Francisco in 1983.

Thank you, Karen, thank you Don. (by the way, this section flowed out in 1500 words)

1.4 I Know

I know what it is like to live in fear. I know what it is like to be afraid to leave my apartment; losing the ability to walk my dog all the way around the block. This was a big problem and a terrible way to live but my emotional prison was much bigger than my physical one. My concept of myself, of who I *was*, and what I *was* capable of, was stuck behind bars—jammed into a very small room. The worse part about it: it *seemed* real. I came to believe that is who I was—not just a situation I was living in, but the essence of who I *was*.

This is a very big problem. Once we are living in a tight compartment, with a small, tiny image of who we are; then we start to make choices about how we behave, what we think, actions we take, and how we treat others. We become very serious, but not about serious stuff. We become serious about things that don't matter. We do this as a way to justify our predicament, make us feel better about ourselves, to improve our self-worth, and to feel like we are not trapped inside that prison. It's a terrible thing to admit to ourselves, let alone others, when we cannot see a way out. Or worse, we absolutely believe the lies we think about ourselves, about our smallness. And when this happens, we have to do something to combat it.

So we act like bullies, we start to control people and situations. We create dramas that make us look important and necessary—all trying to fill a hole that we don't even know is there. This too is a real problem: One that we have and don't even know when we have it. We start to tell ourselves that 'they' are the problem: The people we work for, the people who work for us, our families, and our friends. I have done all of this before. I went ten years without talking to any of my family or close friends. I did so to try and save my life. I did it to feel important, or to claim some power or self-worth. I did it to draw attention to myself; to make myself special and noticed. Imagine needing to cut everyone off in order to get attention. I did so to counter the fear and self-doubt that was raging inside of me. It didn't work so well. It left me more fearful, more doubtful, and more alone. It sucked. I don't recommend it. Some of you may not be going to the extremes I did, but none-the-less you too are isolating yourself, overreacting about stuff, being demanding, controlling; lacking spontaneity, joy, and a deep sense of belonging to others. You too may be trying strategies to combat your weakness with diets, exercise, long hours of work, lots of important commitments, rushing around, complaining about your spouse, telling people how little time you have, and how much you have to do. It may show up in the form of back pain, serious illness, or justified anger at an uncaring spouse. The forms we use to create this life are endless, but at the core, we are attempting to combat the fear that we are not good enough—that, at the core, something is wrong with us. I know this very well; having lived it way too long.

1.5 Stop?

Why would you want to stop yourself from something you do well? What could be dangerous about being a really good singer, or really smart, or even a really nice person? Aren't these the things we aspire to? But what if it isn't the thing itself that is dangerous? What if the danger is in how people might react to you? How do people's reactions to you make you feel? How have people reacted to your gifts, your talents, and your joys in the past? Were they thrilled, joyous, and supportive? Were they concerned, jealous, or intimidated by you? Did it give you more attention than you wanted? Did people actually begin to turn away from you? Did you feel pressure to live up to some standard? Let's get to the heart of this matter. We aren't just talking about any people; we are talking about the people closest to you: Your parents, your siblings, your family, your teachers, and your friends. These relationships form a much stronger bond to you than the world in general. The opinions, actions, and behaviors of these people have a significant impact on *your* interpretation of *your* own self-worth. But the problem here is not them, although I spent many years blaming them for my problems. The problem again rests in our feeling as if we're not good enough. The *not good enough* is actually not related to our talent as a singer, skier, artist, or student. The *not good enough* we are talking about runs much deeper. It runs at the core of who we are. Again, we don't *think* we are good enough, at the essence of ourselves. Our core person isn't good enough. The skiing, singing, and studying is just the surface.

The activity is just the surface…

Here is how it works. Because you are walking around with a wounded core—a core belief that you are not enough, that you are tainted, not up to snuff—then any rebuke, criticism, or judgment goes right to your core. It validates your burgeoning belief that you are not good enough. It's as if your inner voice is saying, 'See? I told you so.' The opinion of the other people is validating your own self-belief—more proof. When these comments come from people with whom you are close, then their opinions ring even truer at your core. It's like being close to a bell that is ringing. The sound is louder. You can feel the vibration much stronger and the impact is greater. Even the positive comments can take a negative turn. When your DNA is screaming 'not good enough,' a positive comment can be construed as 'I have to keep it up' or 'I can't fall off.' Too much of your self-worth is riding on this positive. Since you're not good enough, you need this positive affirmation because you are incapable of validating yourself.

How could a negative validate you and help you feel positive? Because we look outward. We develop the habit of looking outward for an inner validation. This, of course, is impossible. No amount of outer validation can achieve what we are really looking for: Inner acceptance. The self-knowledge that we are okay, we are enough, we are good enough. Even achieving that positive validation—while it feels good at first—won't satiate the inner desire. It only makes us need more, so we seek more. The pressure is now on to achieve; to keep it up. If you slip up, the approval slips and so does your sense of okay-ness. This breeds over-achievers. Because, at your core, you know that you are not getting the nourishment that you really want—inner acceptance—so, even as you achieve more and receive more accolades, you know that you are still starving. But you can't stop. You are afraid to stop. Because then, again, you'd have to face the reality of not being enough. You'd have to face those voices. It's over-eating of a different kind. You do get bloated; bloated with ego. But it doesn't work. It doesn't give you what you need. Now you are really screwed because struggle is your only answer. You need to struggle. You need to show people how hard you are working to achieve your success. At first, success comes easy. It should, because you are gifted and you are playing at your gift; whether you're a gifted athlete, singer, or communicator. The success comes easy. But, since you are looking to get validation from your achievement and you're never satiated; you need more. People won't acknowledge your ease, but they will acknowledge your struggle. *Look how hard he worked. Look at what she overcame. It hasn't come easy for her.* Accolades, all of them. These are what you are seeking. And so are your admirers. By validating your struggle, they validate their own. It makes their struggling okay; worthwhile. Everyone benefits. You no longer need to feel guilty for your ease, or for your gifts. Now you may choose another route. If the giftedness routes don't work, go for the real struggle.

You can do this by dedicating yourself to activities that are outside your giftedness. This is a brilliant strategy, because now you truly do have to struggle to achieve a level of success. But this is better because the pressure is off. You don't really have to achieve any success because your success is accompanied by the struggle. Since this activity isn't in an area of your giftedness, the struggle comes naturally. You have to struggle to even do it. Now you don't have to reach any real heights. People will simply acknowledge you because you're struggling at it. That is the highest form of complement and achievement. Now, if you struggle really hard, you may actually get good at the task—perhaps even excel. Now you are on Easy Street. You get the rewards of struggle and the honor of achievement as well as something more: the exponential reward that results from achievement through struggle—a double whammy. Now we are onto something. But not really, because this too can only last so long.

As we know, this strategy is empty because it does not address the real issue—the realization that you simply are enough, you simply are loved, and you don't have to earn it. You are enough. All this strategy leads to is what every addiction leads to: upping the ante; the need to struggle more to get the same hit. More struggle. But this too ceases to work over time—the hit doesn't come; but we keep trying because we can't stop. That is the definition of addiction. We can't stop even though it doesn't work. We just struggle more. It becomes a way of life; the struggle gets deeper, into our patterns of living, into our choices, into our fate. It gets into our bodies. It shows up in anxieties, depression, accidents, and broken bones. It drives deeper into our longing for acknowledgement, for being enough. But we get caught up in the addiction, so it goes deeper—creating a more powerful disease, more attention, more pain, more struggle. It literally can kill you and it often does. You know this. We may not want to acknowledge it, but we all know the truth. It just doesn't work. No matter how much pain we choose, it just doesn't work.

But, if we are fortunate; we will change and grow more in love with ourselves. As we feel loved, as we feel okay, enough; then we can return to our ease and to our gifts. We no longer need the struggle, because we feel okay. We can return to our ease. And, instead of feeling validated, we get to feel gratitude. Gratitude for the gifts we have been given. Gratitude for being able to play in our gifts and gratitude for receiving the benefits of those gifts. We no longer need to be driven by the needs of the ego to get outer validation or to prove our worth through our accomplishments. We are free. Free to acknowledge our gifts, free to appreciate the contributions of others in our lives, and free to truly appreciate ourselves. We are free from needing to seek *enough-ness*, for we know that we are enough.

I have many examples of trying to do something that I don't really have talent or passion for—examples of running away from my natural gifts; my ease is not ok. I'm unknowingly stuck into a belief system that *hard* is valued and *ease* is wasteful. I'm going to run away from my ease; from my gifts. My underlying motivation was a good one—attempting to find a meaningful life. The problem was that I was doing so with a strategy that was harmful and pain-filled. I was trying to be a good boy; a good soldier. I just didn't realize the cause I was fighting for was rooted in *not good enough*; in trying to prove my *worth*. This is the addiction to struggle in action. Unknowingly choosing pain and frustration and at the same time missing out on life acceleration and the full use of my talents and passion. Not only do we hurt ourselves, but we hurt others by not sharing the gifts and talents we have.

Wouldn't the world operate more beautifully if we were unleashed into our abilities, our passion and our gifts? I'm not the only one caught up in this and neither are you. We have a whole society of people stuck in affliction; in an underutilization of talent. How can we possibly be fully nourished if we are cutting off the full flow of genius that is in each of us? Many of us are operating far below our ability and at the same time expending much energy in struggle. Our struggle has a detrimental impact on ourselves but also on the quality of life on this planet. We are robbing ourselves. It just doesn't make sense. To what extent is our addiction to struggle causing major life afflictions: personal pains, sorrows, lack of meaningful relationships, physical ailments, boredom, anger, frustration, fears of all sorts? What about larger societal issues: crime, murder, diseases of all kinds, unemployment, racism, hunger, wars, and conflicts in all areas of our lives.

I spend my days consulting to organizations. I wonder how much under achievement do we accept. In Jim Collin's book, *Good to Great*, he opens with a powerful comment. 'Good is the enemy of Great.' How low are our standards of success; for ourselves, our organizations, and our society. If so many of us are pursuing life strategies that are in contrast to our fullest expression of life, then our collective measures of success are going to be low. We have no idea the price we are paying; how much joy, success, and achievement we are missing out on.

1.6 Happy God

My teacherfriend, Stanley, gave me a meditation to play with. One of the phrases said that our purpose in life is to enjoy life. I loved reading this line but inside it felt wrong to me. Fortunately I spoke to Stan about how I felt. "I can't buy into this one Stan." From what I see and experience, there is much pain and suffering. How can our purpose be to enjoy life? That seems too shallow. Too superficial. Stan told me that is an old belief system I have. That our recovery is based on an active change in our ideas and beliefs. In that moment I realized that this too was just a belief I had. Not necessarily true. Just a belief. I believe that happiness is superficial. It was a liberating moment for me. I realized that my belief was linked to my assumption, my belief of God and what God wants for us. I still believed that God wants us to experience hardship. It truly was a liberating moment in my life. One of my most liberating. It gave me freedom; detachment. Wow this isn't necessarily true. It's just a belief; an idea. Then a new idea hit me. One that I never had before. I had the idea that God was happy. God was happy. It gave me a giddy feeling inside. A smile; A smirk. It never dawned on me that God was happy. 'God was happy.' I am the creation of a happy God. I am the creation of a happy God. I am the creation of a happy God.' Wow. This was the first time I had even thought this. It wowed me. Then I went a step further. 'I am the happy creation of a happy God. I am the happy creation of a happy God.'

This was; and is revolutionary to me. As I dwelled on this thought it dawned on me that as I see God, so I see my myself. When I use the word *God* here, for me I mean the big guy/girl upstairs. But it's more than that. Here, God represents our highest belief about the purpose of life and our purpose: Our highest ideals of right living. Here's what hit me so powerfully. As I believe so I live. As long as I see *God's* purpose as struggle, then my ultimate purpose is struggle. I was not even aware that this aspiration was running in my system, but now I saw it. We each have a picture, a model of what is our highest purpose. It may not be the one running on the surface of your thinking. It is running deep inside of us, beyond the surface of our conscious thinking. This concept is brilliantly described by Robert Kegan and Lisa Laskow Lahey in their book *Immunity to Change*. Theirs is the best description I've ever seen. For me, they wrap up the book in one sentence: '…we are systematically working against the very goal we genuinely want to achieve.' (p.47) We have a hidden belief system that is contrary to what we think we believe.

I want to play with the word *salvation*. That word may bring up all kinds of religious connotations for you. But let's broaden it a bit. Let's reinterpret *salvation* to mean your beliefs about your ultimate destination, your ultimate purpose, the things that will bring the big freedom; the ultimate rewards of a life well lived.

We can play the same game with the word *Heaven*. Let's imagine that the word *Heaven* represents the ultimate achievement of your best self. What do you believe will get you to Heaven? Maybe you believe that following the Golden Rule will get you there. But under the surface of our conscious thinking, we are each running on a set of beliefs. It took me a lot of work to come to see the beliefs that were running me. I came to realize that I was running on a system based in 'struggle is good'. Suffering and struggle will produce the good stuff. No Pain, No Gain. It is quite shocking to realize. On the surface I want happiness and joy in my life, but under the surface was the Struggle Rule. I was telling myself that struggle would get me to the Promised Land. Struggle would get me respect from others. Struggle is what is needed to achieve my goals. Struggle is what is respected by God. If I want to complete something, then I need struggle. Without struggle my accomplishment are meaningless. I watched myself making things harder than they had to be. In the face of good things, somehow, I'd end up with struggle. If I had a good relationship with a really good woman; I'd mess it up. I'm having fun and success in San Francisco; time for some panic attacks. I'm working on a project; get up tight. I'm about to achieve something really good in athletics, time for an injury. Our business is starting to take off and all of a sudden it starts to tank. My struggle was showing up in all areas of my life because deep inside I believed it was necessary. If I was going to achieve anything worthwhile, I had to struggle.

Whatever we believe is our highest purpose will manifest throughout our whole lives. I had to change my belief about what that highest purpose was. For me that was *God*. It was very powerful to realize the connection. It gave me a sense of control and empowerment. I could change the whole quality of my life by changing my belief about what my highest purpose wanted. I realized that I had to change that belief, otherwise I'd be swimming upstream. I could change small elements of my life, but if I really wanted to change my essential experience, then I'd have to go the source of that river. I was tired of feeling unsettled and unhappy. I was meditating every day and doing much work in an attempt to change. Until Stanley and I talked, it never dawned on me that I had to change my belief about what God wanted for me if I was actually going to change.

I realized that I was designed for joy; designed for success; designed to thrive; to live; to flourish. Un believable. A total change for me. Imagine how powerful this change of belief is for me. Especially knowing that it was these beliefs that were dictating the nature of my life. I was designed to be happy; to fulfill my dreams; to live a good healthy life. Wow. I once went to see Dr. John Mercola speak. I am a big fan of his work on health. I got my money's worth in his first sentence. "We are designed to be healthy." Wow. His message was in conflict to the deep messages. My beliefs tell me that it's our nature to be sick and get serious illnesses; disease is our norm. I became excited to think these new ideas. "We are born to succeed." This feels wonderful, exciting, and exhilarating. At times, I still wonder, 'Can this be true? Am I buying into some hogwash?' My positive beliefs are still in the growing stage. But for Stanley, it's beyond belief. He tells me, "Evan, I don't believe this, I know it." For now, I'm going with his knowing.

1.7 As We Believe, So We Live

I read a lot of concepts that suggest that it's not the circumstances of our lives that determines the quality of our lives. It's our belief system; the way we think. It blows my mind to realize that my beliefs about *God, salvation,* and *Heaven* are determining the success in my work life, my family life, my health, my life—all based on a belief system. It gets better. We can change our belief system. It's malleable. We can adopt new beliefs. If we want to change the quality of our lives; then change our beliefs. I was sitting in meeting yesterday. I was feeling unsettled inside. I started to ask myself some questions as a way to find more peace and to understand what I was telling myself. 'What do I need, what am I asking for, what needs attention, what is on my mind, what action do I need to take, what actions do I want to take?' As I go through these questions I often get clarity; answers. 'Are there beliefs I need to change.' When I'm feeling this way, it feels like I'm clogged, like there is a clog in my life force plumbing. I need and want to unplug it. In this moment I was guided to change my beliefs. When I'm feeling clogged up I don't hear the belief systems running in my mind. They are quiet as words, but I'm learning to feel their presence in my body. So quietly in my mind I started to choose new beliefs; ones that would free me up. 'I am happy, I am positive, I trust that good things are happening, my faith is strong, life is good, God is working in my life right now.' It is not my nature to think like this. I have to purposely and consciously change my thinking; cultivate it. I raised my hand and shared with the folks how I was feeling; what I was doing. This too helps me move my energy; get unclogged; get the clarity I seek. I explained my thought training process; that I need to practice thinking differently, just as a child learns to write. At first, they can't. But they do it over and over and learn how to write. It is such a gift to be able to change and train our thinking. Especially if we can change our lives by changing our beliefs. How wonderful to know this?

Do you know what beliefs are running under your surface? It's kind of simple to see. Take a good look at your life, all of it. Let's make believe that your life, as it is, is the sum total of your beliefs. I hope this makes sense. Imagine that, as we believe so we live. As I believe so I live. James Allen describes this beautifully in his book *As A Man (Woman) Thinketh*. He suggests that every thought we have, every belief is a seed that is planted. Every seed comes to life. If you want to know what you are planting, look at your garden. The source of your frustrations? Your beliefs. The sources of your plenty? Your beliefs. Your wealth, your health, your relationships, your happiness? Your beliefs. It's the ultimate formula for taking responsibility for our lives. The good news? If I really want to change my life, then I need to change my belief system. What I realized with Stanley is that in particular my beliefs about God/Higher Purpose has a great impact on the character of my life. It sounds simple; and it is. But it's not easy. Based on my own experience and of those I study, it truly is a lifelong experience. My friendmentor, Bob, reminds me that we are human. This is our journey. If we had it all figured out, we wouldn't need to be here anymore. Imagine this: God wants me to be happy? Happiness is a valid and powerful way to live? Wow!

> *God is happy*
> *I am the happy creation of a happy creator*
> *God wants me to be happy*
> *I am happy.*

1.8 Leashed

I could pursue a play-filled meaning inspired life as much as I wanted but I wasn't going to be successful because of this underlying commitment I had to struggle. This is why I wrote this book. I want to talk more about play-fullness. What it means for people personally, in our families, in our work, and in our society. I want to talk about play at its finest. Why play is needed for the most important things in life. I truly want people to become more playful; to more fully unleash our talents, our abilities, and our happiness in all areas of our lives. But for people like me, it just won't work if we don't deal with our addiction to struggle. We won't be able to liberate ourselves to truly play if we are still tethered to our struggle. It just won't work.

I was living my dream of *retirement*. I was in San Francisco, the place of my dreams, but I was caught up in something I couldn't understand. All the markings were there of a dream life. If you took a picture of me, trying all these jobs, riding around on my Vespa, it would look great; it's the greatness I imagined. But it wasn't working. I was caught up on the inside. The opportunity was right in front of me and I couldn't enjoy it. My addiction, still unknown to me, had taken hold, was playing itself out on me, sucking away my freedom and my joy. It would take me a long time to see this and whole lot more time to start freeing myself from its grips. Trust me, it's a daily activity to this day and the greatest journey of my life—finding myself again; my freedom; my joy.

1.9 Who's There?

My friend Donald used to tell me that, "Fear is knocking at the door; fear is knocking at the door, fear is knocking at the door; answer it and see that nothing is there." The fear of finding out that I really am not good enough is terrifying, but as I have heard, 'God don't create crap.' If we choose to open the door, be prepared to go BOOOOOOOOOOOOOO! It's one big lie that has captured and imprisoned us.

1.10 Sing a Song

If you had to think of a song that described how you were feeling, what might it be? *I'm a Loser, Englishman in New York, It's Been a Hard Day's Night*? Well, what if we were always playing some song—one created by the collective vibrations of our thoughts, mindset, and emotional state? The way we are walking, the energy and speed of our driving, our fingers typing on the computer keyboard—each pounding out a beat, carrying and reinforcing our mood—whether it's one of agitation, doubt, hope, or happiness. Well, let's play the game in another direction. Let's think of the song we'd like to be playing that would show how we'd like to be feeling, thinking, and behaving? How do you want the texture of your day and work to go? Would the song be: *Love is in the Air, So Happy Together, Somewhere Over the Rainbow*? Pick a song and start playing it. You are the instrument. So, start humming it, walk with its cadence, put its expression on your face, type with its mood in your fingers—literally become the song—the tune, the mood, the message. Heck, we could become our own DJs. Let this be a day of song. Why not choose a song of joy? Gandhi was actually misquoted—what he actually said was, "Be the song you seek to sing."

1.11 Enthusiasm Will Get Me in BIGGG Trouble

One day when I was about 5 years old, my Mom and I were out shopping at Gimbel's Department Store in Philadelphia. She bought me a pair of plaid shorts that I thought were really cool. I was so excited to try them on. As soon as we got home, I ran upstairs to my bedroom and got a pair of scissors to cut off the label. Instead, I mistakenly cut into the pair of pants—right on the front of the leg. I felt upset, ashamed, and embarrassed. It didn't dawn on me that I was still new at this scissors thing. Looking back, my mind made a decision. I better not trust my excitement—if I do, I will mess up something I really care about and get in trouble. While I remember this particular experience vividly, I know I made this same assumption many more times in my life. Decision after decision, I created an anti-excitement instinct. On a deep level, I still carry around the belief that 'if I get excited, I will lose control and cut a hole in my new pants, or screw up a relationship with a client, or ruin our finances, or get in trouble with some authority whose approval I'm seeking'. Again, that's *not good enough*, this fear of making a mistake. By the way, I make mistakes when I'm not excited, or even when I'm downright miserable. But somehow it never dawned on me to be afraid of being miserable.

Since I'm not good enough I need to get some *good enough*. This is struggle, of course, but it's also another attempt to get it from the people I respect or look up to. In this case, my Mom. In business, it's clients who pay on time, or people who work for me, or a boss. I need their approval to fill my *not good enough*. I act out on my excitement. It's my excitement, but it may not be theirs. When I do something, and they get mad, or reject me, or don't give me approval, what I did must go away and must be dangerous because I acted on my own gusto and instincts, and it got me bad reviews and the opposite of approval. It got me damaged. And since I need their approval, I better stop doing that other thing. I better not do what gets me excited and enthusiastic. In essence, I can't trust myself. I don't trust myself and, therefore, I shut down my uniqueness, my enthusiasm, and my vision. These things can only get me in trouble. I know that I am not alone. But if we take this play thing seriously, it's going to be hard to truly unleash it if we are afraid to get excited, feel love, enthusiasm, or hope. Our playfulness is going to touch off rampages of these kinds of feelings, along with creativity, authenticity, and intimacy—some of the other experiences that terrify us. So what the hell are we to do about this? How do we use play to help us heal from our misguided protection systems?

> *I can't screw it up.*
> *I don't have to figure it out.*
> *Everything is working.*
> *All is Well.*

1.12 What it Would Look Like

I'm so excited to get up this morning. I love hearing the birds and the wildlife that surrounds us; especially the running water of the creek. The windows are wide open, and the fresh air is phenomenal. I get up and walk right out the back door for a walk in the meadow. Some mornings I hop on the motor bike, sometimes the mountain bike, and sometimes I go and jump off the rocks into the lake. Now that is an awesome way to welcome the day.

Often, I go right into the workshop. I love to tinker and make stuff out of wood, build new furniture, sculptures, or design new buildings. Some mornings I'll work on a movie, make clothes, or cook up some breakfast concoction.

I'm joined by Dylan, Daniel, or Andrew and we work on stuff together, and my favorite time is when we are in the same space and each of us is working on our own stuff. "Hey, Dad, look at this." I love the sharing of ideas, of space, and of passion. Today I am flying off to Honduras. It is a great flight. I'm meeting with a few activists who have asked me to help them and the government figure out how best to use six gazillion acres of land. They treat me like a King there. We will spend time romping around the jungle, meeting with locals, and having a blast. I will be gone about a week. When I return we are heading out to Jackson Hole for a few days of skiing, and then we're off to New Mexico. The desert is amazing. I always love being there. Tara and I are leading a few retreats. The people are amazing: powerful, open, and fun to be with. They love being with us: hearing about play, meaning, and making real shit happen in the world. The words that describe my life are: vibrant, alive, crisp, crackle, open, free, meaningful, and fun. My gratitude is amazing. This is the life I imagined; it's even better living it.

We have no control over the thought that pops into our heads. Now comes the question: What will we do with that thought? In our world, that thought is a toy; something to play with. How are we going to play with that toy? What game will we play with it?

If we go into the struggle game, then we will worry. We will dwell on it, fret over it, get mad, or build upon it with even more worrying thoughts. I will start juggling more doubt, more worry, and more anxiety. But, at any time, I can change the game and start playing the hope, faith, or trust game. These are all aspects of freedom, of lightness and joy—games of ease and love. Most naturally we will, at any given moment, slip back into a game of worry. Generally, we swing back and forth between worry and hope, but we can choose to spend more of our time on the side of confidence and trust. The game is on, it never stops. The game is not just played in our heads. It migrates in and throughout our bodies. In worry, my body is harder, my jaw clenched. I can become aggressive or I can go the other way, becoming timid, removed, and my body flaccid. It will affect how I dress, how I walk, and the words I choose to describe how I am feeling. Typically, in worry mode, I can use words and phrases like 'overwhelmed', 'I can't stand it', 'there's too much to handle,' and 'when the fuck will this end?' In hope mode, an overwhelming thought might be replaced with being ready, willing, and able. Even my eyes will change. I had a yoga teacher who talked about looking through softer eyes. Literally, my gaze hardens under worry. The furrows on my brow increase and I can become disconnected and isolated. I may be in your company but I'm not really listening because my mind is running through thoughts, strategies, and 'what do I do's?'

I have always lived in abundance. I am living in abundance right now. Everything is as it should be. We have everything we need. We will always be taken care of. All is well…. Really well!

2

The Making of Not Enough

2.1 Big Fat Liar

I am a big fat liar. You are too. You do it at the grocery store, at work, even in your own home. We do it all the time. And guess who we are lying to? Ourselves. Think of all the crap you tell yourself. 'I didn't do a good enough job; I should have said something else; I didn't say the right thing; I don't eat well; I'm not exercising enough; I'm not doing a good enough job at keeping the house clean; I'm too fat; I'm not a good enough Mom; I should be doing more for others.' Lies, lies, lies. Here is the biggest lie of them all. It lingers behind all of the other lies, feeding them and encouraging them to come alive. The biggest, fattest lie of all is the *I'm Not Good Enough* lie. It manifests itself in all of the other crap we tell ourselves. It hides, it's a coward, it doesn't want to show its face directly; it's insidious and penetrates all areas of our lives. It causes us unnecessary hardship and motivates us to work harder than we need too. We beat ourselves up in a strange way for honoring this lie—and most of the time we don't even realize we are doing it. So today, let's worship another God—how about a God who thinks we are great, wonderful, terrific, lovable, and kind? This God's name is *Enough*—the God of Enough. When we worship this God we are good enough, smart enough, happy enough, talented enough, giving enough, caring enough, hardworking enough, and, in doing so, we are blessed with enough—enough money, enough food, enough love, enough joy, enough health. We feel like we are good enough, happy enough, content enough. Have you had enough?

> *"Most people do not expect their path to great abundance to be one of ease and of joy. They have been taught that struggle and hardship and sacrifice are requirements that must be met before the reward of great abundance can be realized. Most do not understand that the very struggle they deliberately involve themselves in, in their quest for success and advantage, actually works against them."*
>
> —*Esther Hicks; aka Abraham*

2.2 Why Am I Making This Harder?

Have you ever asked yourself; why am I making this harder than it has to be? Usually I just experience things as hard, challenging, or frustrating. It can be a visit to the doctor, an argument with my wife, a torn Achilles tendon, a lack of finances, or my back going out. The list can go on and on. On the surface, these are simply the things we deal with in life. One way of making them hard is to get caught up in them—caught up in the drama that they can create. So, on one hand, you have the event itself—like getting stopped by a cop for a speeding violation. That is an annoyance; a difficulty. Then there is our reaction to the event. We can get pissed off, we can feel like a victim as in, 'Why does this type of thing always happen to me?' or we can get frustrated by the process of dealing with the ticket—the cost, the insurance, the handling of extra paper work. We can tell our friends about the situation; reliving it over and over. All of this creates *hard*. And again, on the surface it all seems like normal behavior. But in the midst of this hard stuff, do you ever ask yourself, 'Why am I making this hard?' Forget the ticket itself. What about your reaction? Do you make it harder by getting pissed off or playing the victim stuff? Do you add to the hard by telling your friends and reliving the incident? Do you add even more hard to the situation by letting yourself make the paper work a big deal or getting worried about the additional money? Each of these reactions contributes to your experience of hard. You have just turned a ticket into a hard, a struggle.

But wait, it doesn't stop there. Now it's time to get really serious with this stuff. Have you ever looked at the ticket itself and asked yourself very honestly, 'Why would I want to make my life hard?' Why would you attract and create the experience of getting a ticket in the first place? Now this may sound outlandish and farfetched to some of you. To others, you will get it. Because this is how deep this addiction to struggle runs. It is totally insidious. We literally create and attract situations of hardship. Then on top of that we add more to it to build the drama and make it even harder—more of a struggle. We are so addicted to struggle, we need it so badly, just like we need air, that we will create struggle out of nowhere. This may sound ridiculous, but until we start asking the question; until we understand the need we really have; then we will keep creating these situations and continue to add more stuff on top of them.

I had started getting in shape again; I had hit a really good stride in my workouts. My attitude was great and I was in a groove. One night at the gym I realized that I could literally take it easy—run, workout in ease. As a matter of fact, the easier I took it, the better results I achieved, the more joy I was experiencing. This made it easy to keep it up. I made a commitment that night, to just keep it easy. Especially with my running. Well, the next morning we were setting up for a retreat. We were all set up—and I took some stuff back to the car. The car was parked about 200 yards from the front door. I put the stuff in the car, and feeling peaceful and excited for the retreat, glad to be done in plenty of time, I start heading back to the door. I start to jog and then the idea hits me to sprint—extending my legs and feet all out—and so I do. It felt great; and then twang—I felt a light pull in my Achilles. It wasn't enough to create the great pain of a full tear but it gave me enough pain to change my workout routine and my movement in general. The easy flow of movement that I had accomplished; the arrival that I had celebrated and committed to the night before, was injured—a *hard* was now introduced and an *easy* was changed. So why would I do that? Why would I make this harder? Why would I sabotage the ease that I had achieved, earned, and accomplished? Was it simply an accident? Was it simply a bad decision? Heck, it could have been a positive risk I took. But I have come to see it as my need to struggle. I needed to make it hard or was it because I wasn't yet ready to accept and live with the ease?

We do this all the time. We do it at work. We do it with money. We do it with the peace and ease we achieve in our family lives. Unknowingly, we will screw it up. We don't always blow it wide open, but simply screw it up a little. For some people, I notice serial events of illness. I have witnessed so many people work toward a goal and, when on the verge of completing it, or even after accomplishing it, they get injured. Look at your own life pattern. How many times have you gotten injured, hurt your back, or had some illness, either right before you accomplished something you have been working for or right after you have achieved some goal. Why would you do this to yourself? What purpose does it achieve? Is it simply an accident? Is it simply a coincidence or is there something deeper, more insidious—a pattern going on here?

I can make a list of these incidents in my own life history and I bet you can do the same. When I first started becoming aware of what was going on, I wanted to reject it. You may too. It is hard to accept that you are causing your own difficulties: That you are sabotaging your own success; especially after you have worked so hard to get there. 'This can't be happening. Why would I do this to my-self?' These two pieces are critical and important to acknowledge. The first is the awareness. Maybe it starts as an inkling. 'Could I possibly be doing this?' The first hint. Like the first sniff of an aroma. This may grow to be more confident. 'I think I am creating struggle.' You may live in that question for a while; it may even be years before you build to a full course acceptance and awareness of, 'Oh my God, I am creating my own trouble.' It takes time for one to become aware of, let alone accept the fact that you are addicted to struggle. Imagine your own 12-step program in your head. The first time you tell yourself; 'Hi my name is Evan, I am addicted to struggle.' The second question you will start asking yourself is obvious; 'Why would I do this? Why would I want to create struggle in my life? Why do I want to make this, my life, this project, this achievement, so hard?' Once you are willing, or even excited to ask yourself this question, then you are definitely on the road to letting go of your addiction. I'm not sure it ever goes away. I don't know if that is good news or bad. I have yet to meet a person who has lost all of their struggle. It seems that the degree of our struggle decreases and that we can generate longer and richer periods of ease, but can we completely release ourselves of this addiction? I'm not sure. Now here is an interesting point I have been taught by my teachers, mentors, and guides in life that pain is a spiritual gift.

2.3 Desperation is A Spiritual Gift

Desperation is a spiritual gift too. It seems that we achieve most of our progress in life when we go through difficult situations. While this may be true, I'm not sure that it is necessary. Could this too be an aspect of our addiction? Oh, by the way, I promised you a list. Here is a partial version of mine. You may want to make your own.

How many hours a week do you work?
Do you really need to? How much do you weigh?

Are you happy with how you eat?

Why would you make eating hard?

How is your relationship with your spouse?

Does it suck right now?

Why is that?

Are you struggling to write a book?

Are you having trouble finding the right job?

Are you stuck in an illness or a series of illnesses?

Have you broken your foot, gotten in a car accident?

Do you still have lots of anxiety, depression, or panic attacks?

Why is this?

How is your money situation?

Never enough?

Do you feel guilty because you have too much?

I'm sure you ask yourself these questions all the time. You may get pissed off by them. You may feel like a victim ('woe is me') or overwhelmed ('this problem is too big for me').

2.4 We Are Not Good Enough DNA

Do you feel guilt over your success? Do you feel like you haven't accomplished enough? Why is that? You have to figure out why this is so. Don't you see the pattern? It's there right in front of our eyes. Do you think this is how we were created to be? Have you told yourself that this is your life—this is your fate. I have. I've told myself this is my fate for many years. It was easier to accept this truth rather than see that I was choosing this stuff. It was easier to suffer than to challenge one of my core beliefs—that I was not good enough. It was easier to suffer than to accept the possibility that I was not good enough. It was too scary, too threatening; to look myself straight on and face the fact that I wasn't good enough. That is it. Right there. It's not even a question—a possibility. We believe that we are not good enough, and that is our big problem. That is the big shit. Say it, scream it, look yourself in the mirror, tell yourself the truth for God's sake. Admit it full out. You believe that you are not good enough. Not good enough, not good enough. That's it—not good enough, I am not good enough, I am not good enough. You get it. We're not talking about being a good enough writer, good enough parent, or good enough sales person. We're talking about the core of our being. The essence of who we are. Our totality. We believe that WE are not good enough. This is a huge problem when you honestly believe that as a person. Your core DNA—you—are not good enough. It crosses everywhere you go, everything you do, everything you try to achieve. It is there. It will show up in your marriage, your friendships, your business dealings, and your hobbies. It will show up in your biggest dreams, your most daring accomplishments, in your greatest moments, in your meditations, while driving in the car, in prayer—it is everywhere. Just like gravity. We can't hide from it in a bottle, in sex, in a magazine, in our hobbies, or in our so-called passions in life. These are really just more forms of denial, more obsessions; more attempts to fill that hole—the hole of *not good enough*. It's with us all the time, lurking, fueling us with this great lie that we are not good enough. All the time we are reacting to it, trying to prove it wrong, we are believing it is true. It stops us from trying things, taking risks, and staying with something long enough for it to come to fruition. It sabotages us when we do move forward, when we are applying ourselves, trying something new, dedicating ourselves to a goal. It's there too—and it will still show its face right when we accomplish our goal or on the verge of getting there.

> *I did not ask for success. I asked for wonder and you gave it to me.*
> —Abraham Joshua Heschel

2.5 Fun is an Attack

Why would you want to play more, why would you want to have more fun, why would you want to have a greater sense of ease, with easier solutions and easier living; if you are committed to struggle? No way. The fun is an attack on your struggle. It is an opposition to it. Fun is like a poison to you—so is happiness, joy, and peace of mind. These are direct oppositions to your goal. See, if you are committed to struggle, then fun is a poison. On the surface you will not be aware of this. Who doesn't want more peace, more joy, more fun in their lives? Of course, you do, but not really—because you have a deeper objective, a deeper commitment, a deeper need to sustain yourself. Your struggle is your life blood—it is keeping you alive—why would you want to give it up? Why would you want to threaten it? As soon as you become happy or light, your life sustaining system will kick in and you will need to find some struggle—you will need to oppose the freedom and ease you are experiencing. What else would you do—attack it?

2.6 God is the Culprit

God is the culprit to our problem of *not good enough*.

Not God actually, but rather our conception of God and our relationship to the divine. That being could be God, a parent, or any authority from whom we feel we need approval: The expectations we believe that we need to live up to; the expectations we place on others. The gap between our current situation and the level of those expectations creates the *good enough/not good enough syndrome*. This gap is the space within which our *not good enough* and our *good enough* germinates and grows.

I guess the extent of our *not good enough* depends on our assumption of what that *God* wants from us. What are the standards we are to live up to? What is expected from us? What are the ramifications of us not reaching that level of achievement? Will we be punished? What is the punishment?

It doesn't even matter what the truth is. What is important is our assumption about *that truth*. The more we accept a loving supportive notion of the divine, our *enough* quotients automatically rise. It's like an automatic raise. For me, it's having a sense of God's grace in my life, to the extent that I believe the gifts bestowed upon me are underserved, not needing to be earned, simply a gift, believing that gift of grace comes along with the gift of breath and the gift of mortal life. This belief—my sense of grace and a loving God, a higher power and spirit—gives me great comfort. Essentially it tells me that I am enough, simply as a by-product of being alive or being God's child. Along with this gift of life, I am coming to believe that I also receive divine support—all the time, ready for the asking—but even better, the grace gift gives me support and encouragement and resources even when I forget to ask for them.

The greater sense I have of the divine's generosity and abundance of love and support and nurturing, the greater my sense of security—the security that comes with knowing that I am enough. From here, I can extrapolate out. Not only am I *enough*, but I work enough, my effort is enough, I love enough, I care enough, and I take care of myself and others enough. I am smart enough, talented enough, respected enough, wealthy enough, and healthy enough. It affects how I see others. Are they good enough, are they living up to my expectations? Are situations good enough: my family, my bank account, the company I work for, the people I work with? Everything around us falls under the scope of *good enough*. The standard of which goes back to my Gods, the sources of my expectations, the markers of enoughness, of my core orientation to life, to myself, to others, to the situations I face every day. As I take these beliefs on more and more, I too begin to believe that yes, I am, I really am enough. I am good enough.

As you can see, it's our belief system that governs much of our enoughness. The divine we believe in, the self we believe in and the others we believe in. If we believe that the world is a hostile place, if we don't trust others, our families, our spouses, and our friends, then we are being driven toward a *not enough* orientation. Do we believe that life itself is kind and generous or do we live in a world that is harsh? The extent of our harshness view is equivalent to our not good enough quotient. Let's see if I can explain how this works.

I'm walking down the street. Consciously or unconsciously, I'm walking with a core orientation that life is a threat; unkind and harsh. I used to wake up each morning with a deep sense that my day was going to be full of land mines. The success of my day would be determined by how many land mines I could avoid—be it rude people or frustrating situations. As you can imagine, this is impossible. It is impossible to go through a day without trivial frustrations and sometimes major ones. So here I go, trying to accomplish the impossible, and guess what? I can't. Now either I can be a victim and live with the *woe is me, what is wrong with me? I am fated to a shitty life,* or *woe is me, I'm not good enough to manage this life thing.* I couldn't even get through my day. It must be me. See? Proof positive that I am not good enough. It rests in the evidence of my day. The anger side can come out in aggressive, pissed off-ness at all the idiots in the world. The ones who can't drive, who don't have any clue of what good customer service is, and the ones who are too cheap to leave a decent tip. On the surface, this may not look like a *not good enough* response but let's dig a little deeper. For real, why is this person really pissed off? Because the world did not give them enough—enough respect, enough money, enough kindness, enough of something. They were not given *enough.*

This is a growing belief, though maybe none of us reach it in totality. The strength of it often comes and goes—in time and over time—not a constant like gravity but more like a weather pattern. We really can't blame God anymore. But God still is the culprit here. God is the source of our *not good enoughness.* Not actually God, him/her/their self. It's really our conception of God that is the culprit here.

2.7 Inner Gnawing

As I sit here writing this, I can feel an inner gnawing. A voice running below the surface that is telling me that this isn't long enough, my writing is not deep enough, I'm not doing a good enough job at explaining this, it's not important or valuable enough. Listening to these voices slows down my hands, sucks a bit of my gusto; prevents me from feeling a sense of accomplishment, pride, or excitement that something wonderful is happening. It sucks all my enjoyment out of what I am doing. I feel tentative, watching my words, holding back the flow of information. It's subtle and yet powerful. I feel rushed, needing to get this down fast—so I don't take the time to think, to digest, to allow the information to flow through; no room for error.

When I'm in *not enough* mode, I feel alone, isolated from others, from the divine, from help, from reassurance, from new ideas. It's an odd thing. I cut myself off from what I actually need. It's a double quandary. On one hand I'm feeling *not enough* and instead of taking action to help me get what I need, I actually take action that makes me even *more not enough*. Our addiction in full gear. I'm actually adding to my not enoughness. In a way I'm telling myself the truth when I say I'm not enough. In reality I truly am not enough—none of us are enough on our own. At the very least we need one another. If you believe in a spiritual perspective, then we, on our own, are not enough. We become enough by the aid of a higher power; a God, our spirit. This, for me is where my enoughness comes from. It also comes from a view point. If I believe that I was created by a loving creator, then I can believe that I am essentially enough. I don't believe God would have created a flawed creation. I'm not sure s/he is capable of that. I am enough essentially because I was created by a loving, divine creator. It would be impossible for me to be anything less than enough. This takes a lot of work, not for the creator but for me to come to realize this. It's the essence of my spiritual life journey, coming to believe and know for myself that I am enough: That I am loved, that I am a perfect creation of a perfect creator. This does not mean that I am self-sufficient or that I don't need help. I, my essence, is enough: Is different than believing that I don't need others, don't need God to help me. Of myself I'm not enough to know everything, to solve everything, to figure out everything. I do need more: More help, more wisdom, more insight. But when I realize that I am enough as a being, then I will more readily reach out for help form loving sources, from sources of help that can help, nurture, and bolster me. But when I feel that I'm not good enough, this prohibits me from reaching out and truly connecting with others who can and will help me in positive ways. If I do reach out, often it will be to folks that will reconfirm my *not enoughness*; that will feed my addiction and my struggle. I will not take the risk to truly connect intimately with someone. I will not truly tell you who I am, I will not share my fears, my doubts, or my hopes. It's too risky—since I'm not enough, you will surely reject me. I can't risk letting you know who I really am. I need to be someone that I think you will respect: Someone I think *I* will respect—so I become inauthentic. Again, reinforcing that I am not good enough, but maybe this other version of me will be good enough—in other's eyes. We are looking for validation from others. This is impossible. As soon as I look to you to validate the value of who I am—then I invalidate myself. I just added evidence to the proof that I am not good enough. Ouch. We are in a quandary. To get out of this alone thing I need to take the risk of letting you know me, just as I am. But I'm afraid that I won't be enough for you. Courage my friends. Courage needs to come into play. Choosing to run the risk of rejection is the only answer. We need to find out that we are enough. Here's the cool thing—taking this action. Taking the risk becomes a building block for our self-esteem and for our self-respect. It is an action in the direction of enough.

2.8 Distractions

The kitchen is a mess, again. There is not enough money in our bank account. I'm doing too much around the house. *She* is not doing her share. This is too much work. The list can go on and on. All of this is real stuff. I can see it. We can feel it. We're not making it up. And all of it is a distraction. It distracts us from seeing the good, the plenty, and the abundance that exists in our lives right now. But this stuff takes our attention. It draws us toward that which is bad enough—but its real crime is that it draws us away from experiencing the goodness that abounds. This too is the act of the struggler. It has to be. It has to feed the struggle. It is a great strategy. As long as we are watching what *isn't enough*, we are blind to what *is enough*. Seeing *not enough* kicks us into actions that come from a place of struggle. This applies, we know, to ourselves and to all the messages and evidence that we see which shows that we are not enough. Now the struggler can add to the struggle by constantly showing us how we don't have enough in our life.

I love and respect myself.
I love and respect myself.
I love and respect myself.

2.9 Afraid to Let Go

I just can't believe that I am truly loved and cared for. I can't believe that I am protected and guided by a loving light at all times. No way, it can't be true. I love the way it sounds, but when we are running out of money, when my parent is seriously ill, when I can't see my way out of a problem, when it doesn't seem to be getting better, when I feel alone and scared; it is really hard to let go, to let go and trust that all is well, that I am on a ship that is sailing, guided in love to a better place, that this is perfect, that we are living perfectly; that love and promise are caring for us. It is really hard.

I feel like I need to stay in struggle, in *non-peace*. In this strain I feel that the anxiety, the fear, the concern, and the anger are my partners. If I let go of them; I will sink. If I move to calm; I will die or perish—or nothing will change. No way will this get better unless I'm in stress. The stress will guide me to take new action, better action; it will get me out of this place. If I stay in calm, I'm screwed—nothing can change in peace. I can't let go. If we let go and let God take control, we're screwed. This will never be solved; no solution will come. We will go down—drowning with a smile. The struggle is my savior; the peace my demise. No wonder it is so hard to let go of the addiction to struggle. I think of it as my savior.

> *Right now! Right now, I am safe.*
>
> *Right now I am loved.*
>
> *Right now I am guided.*
>
> *Right now I am great! We are on the path.*
>
> *It is brilliant.*
>
> *Our guidance is clear.*
>
> *It's okay to be peaceful.*
>
> *It's okay to be sure.*
>
> *It's okay to let go. All is well. Right now!*

2.10 A Rigorous Course

I submitted a proposal to teach an MBA course on *Play*. The working title is *Playing on the Job: A Radical Approach to People, Passion, and Profit*. I want to explore the role of play as a way to redefine what it means to work. If we can remove the element of struggle from our definition of work and replace it with a sense of enjoyment, of passion, of something we desire to do, what would our workday look like? How would we pick our professions? What would it mean to be a *boss*? A whole other aspect would look at our home life. If we give up the struggle element of work, then how do we talk about work when we come home? If we had a great day at work, would that change the way we related to our children, to our spouses, and to our household responsibilities? Not only would this affect our actual compensation for daily action (work) but also our *home work*, our work around the home, and even our volunteer work. All of our work.

Work is one of our hotbeds for struggle. The word itself connotes struggle, hardship, and drudgery. 'Oh damn, I have to go to work.' 'I have to be at work at 7:30 am,' 'work is a real pain in the ass.' It gives us something to talk about with our friends. It's an area of commiseration and an area of life where we can agree that we must struggle. It's like a bath of struggle, a common ground of complaint, a way to indulge in struggle language, energy, and camaraderie. It would really take something for us to give that up. What would we talk about at parties, over lunch, and at the ball game? It may sound like a no brainer to turn work into an area of enjoyment, but many of us aren't ready to do this. We can't let go of the crutch. If we still need the struggle in our lives, then work is a great area to indulge it. Who wants to like their boss, or look forward to going to work, or even have a ball doing our job? The ridicule would be great. It would play into the same ridicule we received as kids growing up. It's just not cool to have fun at school, to sit up front, to raise our hands, and be into it. We got called names like *teacher's pet* for doing stuff like that. As adults, we risk the same ridicule for being a *boy scout* about our work. It's much cooler to be reticent and not give ourselves fully to what we are doing. It takes courage to tell people that we love our work, our wives, our husbands, and our children. People will talk behind your back, claim that you are not for real, are hiding something, or on drugs. So while on the surface, playing at work seems like a great goal, on the inside many of us are terrified to actually do it. We'd have to give up the pay we get from *hating work* or being dissatisfied. Do you realize how much you get out of it? Let's look at some of the struggle pay you do get. You get to have something to talk to people about and thus be a part of the team. It gives us a great way to belong, which, at the core, is what we are all looking for. At a party, you now have something in common, a way to get a sympathetic ear and some caring as soon as you start complaining about work. At home, you now have a great excuse for being alone, or avoiding the family responsibilities. You can complain about how hard work is, how much you still need to do, and thus you get charity points. People give us a break and don't expect as much from us because work is so damn hard. How could I do the dishes, take care of the kids, spend intimate time with my spouse when I just worked so hard?

When I submitted the course, one of the Deans told me that the students were required to take other courses, rigorous ones. Essentially, he was setting me up for the rejection. It was his way of telling me that he didn't think the course would go through because it wasn't rigorous enough. He was absolutely on point. This course was not designed to be rigorous. However, what he was really saying was that rigorous courses translated into valuable courses. Moreover, he was saying that if the course wasn't rigorous—not to mention being downright enjoyable or even possibly fun—then it wasn't valuable. We can't blame him for this misaligned prejudice. He too had been raised in a system—in this case, an educational one—that honors rigor, pain, and hardship: A system that equates this with value, real learning, and meaning. Little did he know the conspiracy he was playing into. This mentality just perpetuated and created more pain, not more meaning or value. It doesn't mean that the students will eventually learn more or gain more value, more practical experience, and more tools to help them be successful at work; or that they will develop better relationships with the other students. It just means that they will get more practice at how to start struggling. The struggle mentally will be reinforced again, and they will be better prepared to go out and struggle themselves in the workplace and at home. They will become better struggle managers and leaders and they will create more dissatisfaction for others. The game will continue. But what the Dean won't teach is that, in enjoyment in our employment, people are unleashed to do their best. Through the lack of struggle in the class, they would gain some of the most powerful insights into life and work. They could be better equipped to handle the real hardships that will come their way. They could be solution-oriented, finding new and creative ways to get things done, finding meaning in their work, and building the dynamic personal networks that would allow them to get their work done, and actually accomplish real goals. This they will miss. Of course, if you asked this Dean if these goals are desirable, he'd say yes for sure. But, at the core, he won't really go for them because he will choose *rigorous* over *joy*. He too needs to go home to his wife, open the door and enjoy the benefits of saying, "Work was really hard, you wouldn't believe what they did today."

2.11 Intimacy

Struggle at work—or in any area of our life—gives us a great escape from this closeness, which terrifies us. Our old friend, *not good enough*, is again the culprit. The reason we don't get close, open up about our true selves, our true desires, or our true joy is that in these states we are vulnerable; our defenses are down. We are letting you know exactly who we are, which makes us vulnerable and thus open for rejection. If I were in this state, not only would you reject me, you'd also reject the real me. When we believe we are not good enough, we need validation from outside of us. We need others to like us, to desire us, to let us know we are good enough. The threat of rejection is too high a risk to take; especially if we are being real; because if you reject me, then you are rejecting the real me. At least if I put up a façade, if I protect myself; then if you reject me, you are not rejecting the real me. It can't be too bad, but if I open my heart, my real me, and get rejected then that is terrible; too high a price to pay.

> *Prayer for Protection The Light of God surrounds me.*
> *The Love of God enfolds me.*
> *The Power of God protects me.*
> *The Mind of God guides me.*
> *Wherever I am, God is!*
> —James Dillet Freeman

2.12 Enough Already

I sure hope that I can explain this. This *Not Good Enough* is insidious. It runs deeply into our everyday. From the core of a *not good enough* root stems many branches. Because, acknowledging we are not good enough, creates the experience that we don't have enough. We don't do a good enough job. The people in our life are not good enough. Our expectations for ourselves and others become out of whack. Since we don't have enough, we want more. *Not enough* expands into our bodies—we are not healthy enough, not strong enough, and not beautiful enough. Our spouses are not loving enough, our kids don't behave well enough. The waiter at the restaurant didn't treat me nicely enough. Every aspect of our lives becomes infected with *not enoughness*. We don't do enough— at work, for our customers, for our families. Our bank accounts aren't robust enough. We become broke, not just financially but psychically, emotionally, and spiritually. This sets us out on a quest to get enough, to be enough. We work harder—or we give up. We can only try for so long, so hard to become enough. And when we don't see any progress, we can be thrown deeper into a compulsion to fill up the enough meter, or we simply give up. It's just not worth trying anymore. It gets worse. Now, again we have reinforced this truth. And it is worse because rarely do we see what is actually creating our unease. We often think it's our spouse's fault—'if only they were more loving to me.'

Sometimes we actually believe we'd be more relaxed if we just had more money in our accounts. 'If my boss would just be more appreciative. If only my abs looked a bit tighter. Really, if my blood pressure was lower, my house neater, my kids more respectful, then I'd feel better.' We don't see what's going on. We keep throwing our hopes and energy into these areas of our life and they don't get better. Or, even if they do, the *hit* of relief is short-lived because some other area of our life goes unfulfilled—and will need more. We just don't see that at the core of our dissatisfaction is OUR *not enoughness*.

Our drive for more leaves us blocked off from realizing what we do have. It blocks us off from feeling grateful. It's hard to be grateful when we feel we are lacking. Our focus is constantly on trying to be enough or get to a state of enough. We think that if we could just fill that void we'd feel better, but it doesn't work. The focus on our lack makes it impossible to see what we do have. It's very hard to be grateful when we feel *not good enough*. It's very ironic, because we learn that the way out of our problem is the pursuit of gratitude. The *more* that we need is more gratitude. And it takes work. It takes real work to draw our attention away from our lack and to focus on what we do have. The addicted part of us craves to look at our *not enoughness* because it tells us that this is where we'll find our solution, but it won't work. It never will. But gratitude will. Gratitude starts us down the road to healing.

2.13 Plenty

Life will naturally give us plenty of difficulty. We don't need to create more. There is plenty of natural struggle—money, physical ailments and disease, family disharmonies, disagreements with co-workers, drivers on the road, grief; the natural challenges that come with change: in age, situations, spirit. There is plenty. It goes on all day long. It will go on for our lifetimes. It's built in too. The struggles are built in as well as into the life thing. We get enough to learn the lessons we need to learn. The struggles, the difficulties, are really important qualities to our growth, to our advancement, to our learning. It keeps life interesting, brings us to new places, helps us learn new stuff, new skills, meet new people, end up in places we could have never imagined. Great places. My whole spiritual life is a by-product of difficulty. It's the difficulty, the discomfort, the pain that I experience that propels me deeper, to learn more about myself, to find new solutions, to deepen into existing ones, to explore new frontiers. The best stuff in my life has come out of difficulty, pain, dis-ease, and disharmony. The most important aspects of my adult life have come from struggle; from the seeking ways out of the pain and frustration, from a search for a resolution to that struggle. We don't need to create more. We don't need to create more struggle.

2.14 Am I Creating Struggle?

Another great question. If we are inclined toward struggle, we can always stop and check. Are we doing it now? Am I making this situation harder than it needs to be? How am I making this hard?

3

A Path to Enoughness

3.1 I Am Enough

I am smart enough. I am talented enough. I am prepared enough. I am ready enough. I work enough. I have learned enough. I am lucky enough. I am kind enough. I know enough. I have enough.

I AM ENOUGH!!!

I am divinely inspired—all of my actions, my thoughts, and my beliefs are fully built, cell by cell, wave by wave, and molecule by molecule, with the building blocks of divine love. There is nothing about me that isn't divine. I am love. I am loved. Every thought, every action, every move is all 100 percent love, perfect, moving, touching, deeply inspired, and meaningful. I can make no mistake; I am not a mistake. I am fine—perfect enough. I am enough. I was created by enough. There are no gaps; not one single gap. Everything about me is enough. I am enough, I am enough, I am enough …. Thank God almighty, I am enough!!

I am enough.

I walk enough.

I talk enough.

I am a good enough parent.

I eat well enough.

I teach well enough.

I am prepared enough.

I have learned enough, worked enough, earned enough.

I treat others well enough.

I care enough. I give enough. I ask enough.

I am courageous enough. I love enough. I clean the house enough.

I dress well enough. I am in shape enough. I give enough.

I earn enough. I am trying hard enough. I work hard enough.

I am having enough fun. I am generous enough. I am happy enough.

My spouse is loving enough.

My parents are good enough.

I have enough money.

My friends are good enough.

I have enough energy. I am enough.

I am enough.

3.2 Give up the Struggle

What do we do with our struggle? It has to go somewhere. But where? I give it up. Up to God. Now you may say that God is also down, over, inside, to the left, and to the right. You might even give your struggle to someone else. Trust me, there are plenty of folks out there willing to take on more struggle. We call them victims. In victim mode, we are willing to take on the struggle of others. We take on their beliefs; we take on their pains, their frustrations, their anger, and their disappointments. But do I really want to expand my struggle by giving it to another? Not only do we create more struggles for others when we give it to them, it also means it doesn't really go away. We end up attracting even more. You know the whole reciprocity thing. What we give is what we get. So it seems that there has to be someone or something we can give it to. It really helps me when I give it up.

When I give my friend, Ralph, a call and tell him how I am feeling, this really helps me in the giving it up process. When I pray and ask God to help me; that helps me give it up. Writing in my journal, sharing with my wife; this helps me give it up. Cleaning the house or going for a walk can each help me give it up. Meditating or doing my movements in water can really help. Sometimes, waiting can help a lot too.

Giving up the struggle is really much bigger. The bigger issue is a decision. A decision to become happy, to become joyous, to become free. My whole spiritual life is in essence a decision to give up struggle and to embrace love, to embrace happiness, to embrace a meaningful life. My friendteacher, Stanley, used the line, "Stop enduring life and start enjoying life." This isn't a one stop deal, it's a life journey. It's one of the main points of this book, that our spiritual journeys are a journey of giving up our struggle, a journey of finding out we are loved, we are whole, we are complete—A journey of finding joy, of finding peace, of finding love and happiness. Our journeys make take many many forms in our own lives. Stanley often speaks to me about finding an eclectic approach. Taking pieces and ideas from many sources and bringing them together to find a path that works for each one of us. This makes sense to me and opens the door for me to find a way that works for me. This, for me is very important, that we each may find our own paths. Our path to find our *enoughness,* to finding out we are loved, is a spiritual path. Our spiritual journey is one of finding *enough-*

ness. This is the essential message of this book. In my life, the only solution to my *not enoughness* is a spiritual solution. Struggle has not filled that void. My spiritual life has. That really is the point of this whole book.

3.3 Secret Agent Man

Today I am going to be enough. Maybe I can hold this for one minute, or an hour, or all day—I'm not sure. But I do know that I sure prefer to live when I am feeling alive, vibrant, my teeth chomping on my day, engaged in what I am doing, free, carbonated, and excited. Underneath these feelings is confidence. It is really hard to play alive when I am feeling timid, worried, concerned, held back, anchored, or tethered by my fears or my sense of lacking. I can wake up feeling tight, hardened and not even know why. So, I lay in bed this morning and meditated. I started by repeating affirmations about how I would like to feel. This is a prayer/meditation game that I often play. It doesn't work all the time, but usually I can tell pretty quickly if it's going to work. I can feel my energy starting to shift as I start to say my affirmation.

> *I am confident. I am proud. I am happy with myself. I trust myself. I am alive and thriving. I am confident and secure. I am thrilled to be alive.*

I go on and on. It's easy because I can quickly think of words and phrases that describe how I would like to feel. I don't have a memorized litany of phrases—I make them up in the moment. I may repeat them for 5 minutes; 10 minutes. Sometimes it lasts for 30 minutes or an hour. Often, I fall asleep again while I am doing this. Time can go quickly. As I am doing this, the other voices will show themselves—the fears, concerns, or worries that I am having will often surface. The nice thing about being in this mode of prayer is that these fear-based voices reveal to me what I am concerned about. I can hear the themes, the common threads. Usually it is nonsense, a sequence of stuff that doesn't matter at all, but that my mind wants to grab on to. I ask myself, if this stuff doesn't matter, then what is its purpose? Why would my mind want to grab on, play with, and think about things that just create, fortify, and support the chemicals of worry in my body, the thought patterns of worry in my body, and the muscle tension that results. When I worry, it has its natural prayer—it kind of works like my affirmations in reverse. As I worry or dwell on one thing, it will naturally lead to another thing to worry about, and then another. A chain of worry. It's a worry party. Like being at a dance club. The DJ playing one dance song after another as we throw our bodies and mind into the songs and keep dancing. This is the dance of worry; of doubt. We are feeding ourselves on a diet of concern, insecurity, and doubt. But why would we do this? Why do we self-generate concern? Why do we crave it? On the surface, who would want more doubt and insecurity? Why would we gravitate toward it? It takes on the form of a hobby. But why? If I were to create myself, I would clearly pick a pattern of security; of hope and light. I would like to believe that in my spare time, or waking up time, that my mind—conscious and unconscious—would get a kick out of dwelling on joy, on hope, and on things I am looking forward too. I would like to believe that I would focus on how well I do things; on how positively a situation would go. I would like to go to a dance party of hope, joy, and positivity. So why do we get caught up in self-doubt and its consciousness of despair and concern? It must be serving some purpose.

Here we go again. Struggle!

We have a need to struggle! We believe that our doubt will help us in some way. We're protecting ourselves in some weird way. It has to be some form of distorted protection and aid. We are totally geared to living; just like plants, trees, and bugs. This mode of negative thinking must have some form of life protection and enhancement built into its DNA. But what is it protecting, what is it promoting, and what is its life-enhancing purpose? The whole reason I am writing this morning is a way to counter a fear voice that wants to keep me curled up; small and timid. But I want to feel engaged and alive like Secret Agent Man: Out in life with a purpose, gusto, and strength. This is my real purpose. And yet, underneath this purpose lurks another, very strong, persistent and brilliant Secret Agent Man.

Somehow, we have a belief that success is dangerous. We have come to believe that we are safe when we are injured and in a state of insecurity. We have learned that feeling disappointed, depressed, and dissatisfied gives us a cloak of redemption. We seek these states as a way to protect ourselves and ensure that we are okay. We are even smart enough not to hear this call, or to see it, or admit it. These goals run under the surface, in hiding, away from our awareness. It's safe that way—undetected it can run wild and strong. This too is one of its strengths. It protects itself so that it can better protect us. I'm not exactly sure how we got this way.

The Greek myths teach us the lesson of struggle. The biblical stories and even the great Disney fairy tales carry this message. There has to be pain, struggle, or disappointment if we are to have redemption and happy endings. What a crock of shit.

Who sold us this bill of goods? There is some very good snake oil salesman running around the universe. It is not my point to figure out where this came from, but rather to identify or play with its existence—to see it, grab it, and decide what we want to do with it. I'm not even sure we can eradicate it or get rid of it. I'm not sure how deeply it is engrained in our DNA of living. I have got to believe that we can loosen its grip and strengthen our desire and ability to live more of our time in ease, confidence, gusto, and joy.

As Secret Agent Man, I see myself writing, out on adventures, engaged in activities. Now I can sit here and write timidly, caught up in the feelings and my thoughts—'is this any good? Will anybody like this? This is dumb.' I can write with those feelings (I often do), but the game I want to play is acting with gusto today.

I wonder if one of the things we can do is not eradicate the fear, the *not good enough*, but counter it by bathing in thoughts of power and beauty and safety. We can read about it, talk about it, write about, and pray about it. We can do our best to act like it and to live it even when we don't feel it. We can want it; desire it greatly. We can strengthen our enoughness, our power, our hope, our faith in our language, how we speak, who we hang out with, what we watch on TV, and what we listen to. We can inundate ourselves with hope and light. We can become as strong as possible—iron men and women of hope. This we do have some control over even if we can't get rid of those voices of fear, struggle, and *not good enoughness*.

3.4 God on a Stick

I got a tennis ball and wrote the word God on it. Then I went to the tennis court and started playing with it—hitting the ball. I was afraid that I was going to go to hell or get punished somehow by the divine for doing this. It seemed so sacrilegious—so against the grain of everything I was taught about God, prayer, and being respectful of the deity—and it was, of course, in the tradition of the great Moses himself. If you mess around with God and go against the grain, then you get punished big time—death and suffering stuff. This is the tradition that I was going against by playing ball with God's name on it—daring to play with the big guy himself. Often it happens that, when I am expanding my boundaries, going against the grain, doing something to let my imagination, my unique view, my different, original side of myself out; I become afraid of reprisal. In high school, I had this fear of getting beaten up. Now there was no evidence that this would actually happen, but my fear was that if I truly let myself out, then I'd get beaten up. The real fear that we all have is of being vulnerable. It takes courage to let our true selves out. It takes courage to play, because in this state of realness, we are unprotected—or so we think. When we are playing for real, then, we can get rejected. And if you reject me when I am playing for real, being the real me, exposing my core, then what you really are rejecting is me—not my ideas, not my feelings; but me. This is risky especially if you are still running on *not good enough*. If you feel, think, or are afraid that you—at the core, your essence—isn't good enough. If you have not figured out that you are good enough, then this rejection can't be protected. There must be some math formula that states: To the extent you know you are enough will relate to the extent you are able to handle rejection and its parallel; your willingness to be yourself.

It was one thing to let myself have the original idea to write God on a ball and play with it. That takes a certain amount of *good enough* juice. To actually write the words takes some juice, to go to the court and play with the ball takes juice, to tell others about it takes even more juice, to announce it with confidence took another twenty years of *good enough* juice development. I have become more confident in myself and in my ideas, more trusting in God, the universe, my life. This has given me more freedom, more room to play with these ideas, to cultivate them, to express them, to even feel driven to share them with others.

One of the things my kids love to eat is pickles on a stick. I get a chop stick from the drawer and put it into the bottom of the pickle. They love it. It's fun for them. I'm not sure they'd be so excited to just eat the pickle. But put it on a stick and now this is fun and tasty. We also put hot dogs on sticks and eat them too. It's fun to do and they get a kick out of it. Then one day we got really wild. I put a hot dog and a pickle on the same stick—one on each end. This was awesome. Now it's the same hot dog as would usually go on a plate or in a bun and the same pickle that would be sliced or eaten whole, but putting them on a stick gives it a whole new vibe, for them and for me. It's part adventure, part breaking out of the normal mold, part originality, part breaking the rules—and simply fun and enjoyable to them. I felt the same way and still do about writing God on a ball, playing with the ball, and calling that prayer. I love putting God on a stick so to speak.

A friend of mine really helped me expand and free up my notion of prayer. She told me that when she thinks of someone, as in the thought of them crosses your mind out of the blue, she considers that prayer. Well this really blew my notion of prayer wide open. It was so far afield from how I was raised: With a set cannon of prayers in a prayer book to be said word-by-word at certain times and accompanied by certain rituals. Her version was so much freer, easier, and expansive. It made prayer so much more accessible to me. This doesn't mean that I still can't pray out of the book, but now I have so many more options. When I get over my fear of divine rejection, for being creative and original in my prayer modalities, then the door opens up even more. This is the power of *Play* in action.

We start to feel comfortable enough to play with anything in our lives. From what dinner looks like, to what prayer looks like, to what a sales call looks like; we open ourselves up to a much wider pallet of expression. We open the door to ourselves—to allowing our own unique vision and version of life to come out. We stop robbing ourselves and those around us of our powerful ways of living, of being effective, of changing the world, of reaching, of learning, and of having fun. We stop navigating the world and our lives from a narrow range of possibility. We open ourselves to new solutions, more kindness, and less struggle. This *not good enough, no-play* way of living is causing a starvation of ideas and solutions on this planet. We are keeping ourselves imprisoned in a world that is much smaller, meager, and starved. We've cut ourselves off from the life force within which breeds life; new life—a vibrant life. We stay mired in a pollution-filled life. Our living spaces on the physical, mental, and spiritual level are so narrow that we are choking ourselves. This lack of freedom, of creating new space, by breathing the same old air of ideas, old ways of doing things, old knowledge, and old information is literally suffocating us. We need new air, we need new space, we need new room to move, we need more food for thought and for living. This life pollution is causing more disease, more strife, more hunger, more anger, more disappointment, more drugs—and all because we are afraid of divine rejection. This is the rejection we fear the most and we're not even aware of it.

This is why we have to play. Not just because it is a fun diversion in life but because we need it to live. We need it in business, we need it in education, in spirituality, in our home lives, on our farms, and in our government. Because where do the new ideas and solutions come from? From someone or some group who is willing to play with how things are getting done, who will experiment, try some new ideas, be courageous, unique, and mostly real. To *not play* is to cut ourselves off from the lifeline; cosmic and otherwise. When we are stuck doing things the way they have always been, playing it safe; we are no longer advancing, growing, escaping, and finding new ways of doing things. Where do new ideas and inventions come from? From someone responding to an inner inkling, an idea, a passion, and a twinkle in their eye. We have all had them—new original thoughts—but *they* have the courage or the desire or enough desperation to try it. This is how we grow; how we live. This is the essence of living—not just getting by and logging in another day. We're talking about living, with zest, with passion, with clarity, and with determination. We have to *Play*.

It's this divine rejection that manifests itself at the surface of my fear of being myself, of being vulnerable, of letting you know who I truly am. Who am I? Who created me? The divine; of course. So when I'm afraid that you will reject me, if you knew who I really am, what I'm really doing is rejecting God, the divine—and rejecting myself. If God created me and I'm afraid to be me, then I'm afraid of God, afraid that I'm not enough. This means that I'm afraid that God isn't enough. If I take the risk to let you know who I am, at the core, I am validating God—the goodness of God—because God created me. I am good enough and it's because God is a good enough creator. If I'm not good enough, then God must not be good enough either.

So let's go back to the beginning. I'm afraid to write God on a ball. I'm afraid to be original, trust myself, or be myself wholly. I'm afraid because I don't trust God. I'm afraid I'll be punished. Here's the key: We need to take that risk. Which is ridiculous because there can't be anything more powerful and less threatening than to respond to that call, that core, that essence, that impulse. It's the safest thing we can do, because this is when we are doing and being who God created us to be. We may talk about the risk or the courage but that is silly; that's just because we've been taught to be afraid. Or we've experienced rejection in our lives from people; people who were disconnected from their core. We scare the shit out of them when we are real because then it threatens them. They smell the realness and know that they want to be real too. It's too scary so they put us down to protect themselves. We all do this but it is just scared humans talking; humans disconnected from their core; not talking to God. We are at our best, most safe, when we take action—whether it's by putting the pickle on the stick or writing God on a ball. This is when we are most aligned and pro- tected by the power, our power, the divine power. If you reject this call, then you are taking sides—taking the side of fear and rejecting the divine. So stop. We are not being rejected by the divine, we are the ones doing the rejecting. So go tell someone you love them. Whenever that voice comes, trust it. It's the best thing we can do for ourselves, for others, and for this planet.

3.5 Play or Pay

We think that play is goofing around. So when we say, "I'm playing too much," that really means that we're goofing around, wasting too much time. Maybe it's worse. We have as- sociated the feeling of freedom, of joy, of working with joy and energy, with goofing around. We have associated rigidity and accomplishing a lot with value and real work. But when we play, we get stuff done much faster and easier. So what might look like goofing around is actually being alive, engaged, and having fun. Being innovative. Being effective. It's just not rigid or linear. It may look wasteful only because it doesn't follow a straight, linear, one- thing-at-a-time type pattern. It's alive, vibrant, and multi-faceted. It wants to pop in and pop out. It looks wasteful only in comparison to what our notion of working hard looks like. It's too bad. Because this *wasteful* goofing around lets us get much more done. It helps us find new ways of doing stuff, and allows us to come away from work feeling nourished, uplifted, and energized. Then we are able to go home and truly engage with our families rather than needing all that time to *regroup*—which is just another word for *isolation* from our families. That scares the shit out of us too—being intimate with people.

So it's better to be rigid while we work so we come home exhausted, with this fake impression of getting a lot done. Now we're too tired to really engage with our families, to be real and intimate with them. And best of all, it gives us a great excuse for another hard day's work. This rigidity allows us to be isolated at home and at work. We can deal with people all day long without having to be intimate and real with them. Better not goof around, because then we are ourselves, our vulnerable real selves; the ones that can connect with people in a real way. The kind of way that energizes us, makes us feel safe, more vibrant, and alive. See this goofing around thing is cool if you are up for great things and a great life. If that is too scary, then keep away from it; call it goofing around and don't do it. Drink heavily instead. Have you ever heard that called goofing around? No, that is called being an adult, and doing business. What a crock.

We are starved for intimacy... really. We may try to reject it but just know that we all want it. This force is unstoppable. This is the God force. We are starved for those intimate moments because they create such a connection; and yet we can be scared of them as well. Sort of like being on a high dive looking down; afraid to jump. Yet, once we do, there is a feeling of relief, of exhilaration, of connection. What stops us from *going there*, toward those intimate moments? Once we experience them they are treasured moments of realness, of connection, and of pure love. Why, when we hunger for them, do we retreat from them? And what if, instead of being few and far between, intimate moments filled our lives with connection and with pure love?

I am loved.

I am loved.

I am loved.

3.6 Jesus Had Fun

When I think of doing *God's work*, the images that come to me are of deprivation—in the sense of poverty, hardship, doing much with little; even suffering. But I can't imagine this is the whole story.

Today, I was sitting here in a prayerful moment. I was playing with images of doing *God's work*. At the time, I was calling folks to invite them to a free leadership program that we do. All day I have been stopping myself before I take action in order to orient my purpose and to establish why am I taking this particular action. The real game I'm playing is a *Love* game. What if I knew, believed, and felt that I was truly loved by the divine? What if I knew that all was well? That all my needs were already met; that everything was fine, wonderful, and blessed? In this game, I have the life force of trees, the brilliance of hawks, and the power of viruses. I've got to believe that, as humans, we have all of this in one bundle and much more.

Knowing that I am immersed in this life force, how would I write that email? Why would I call that person if I knew that I was 100% driven by this life force? If I really knew that I had everything I needed, abundantly, what would I do next? I was about to make one of those calls, so I stopped myself, allowing my actions to be guided by these intentions; this energy. I want to bathe in these ideas before I act. I imagined myself making the call; moving molecules of love, of good enough, and of plenty.

Maybe this person, whose name I was drawn to, needed some of this energy, or a blessing, or attention. Maybe they would be a [life force tennis partner]—we could bounce some life molecules around together. Then I asked myself a great question: Why make this call at all if everything was already taken care of? A beautiful answer came to me. I'm sure it was a result of a conversation I had with my friend, Ed Hastings. Ed and I asked the same question about prayer and meditation. Why pray and meditate if everything is okay? What if doing God's work is what we wanted to do? What if I'm motivated to do it because it is pleasurable, energizing, and fun? Imagine that: God's Work is Fun?

Maybe I do have to do God's work. Not because it is a burden, or demanded of me, but because I enjoy being at peace, alive, playful, and graceful. It's just like an artist who has to create, a kid who has to go outside and play ball—because it's so damn fun and rewarding. I've got to believe that, for Jesus, doing his thing was fun, rewarding, and energizing. At least I'd like to carry that vision with me today rather than just one of burden and hardship. Yes, Jesus had fun. Moses, Buddha, and my Grandma too.

3.7 Fun Is Enough

I'm getting an inkling. The nudge of a voice. That is not true—the inkling started coming a few years ago. I was going on a sales call. I was thinking about my purpose; my intention for the call. I had come to believe that my purpose was to be a missionary of help. This came to me in a conversation with my friend, Bob Megill. Actually, he and I have had a few hundred conversations about this topic. You remember Bob—he's the one who introduced me to the concept of *addiction to struggle*. I once asked him where he got this idea from. I thought he had made it up. Turns out, he had picked it up from someone else. Undoubtedly, they had gotten it from someone too.

When I first met Bob I was caught up in a struggle game with the notion of selling. To me, selling was a profession of manipulation. Words like: Manipulation, disingenuine, dishonest, fake, slick described my sense of what it meant to be a sales person; none of which I wanted to be. It was one of the last things I wanted to do. At the time I met Bob, I was enrolled in a selling course. Based on advice I had received, it seemed that I needed to learn how to sell.

The advice I was seeking came from my *not good enough* sense of myself. Before I met Tara, I started a company called *Emma Productions*. It was mostly teambuilding and some customer service training. The company was growing and then took a nose dive in terms of revenue. At the time I was unclear to what had happened. I assumed that I had done something wrong and I wanted to fix it. I turned to a few folks who seemed to be running successful companies. I didn't know them well and was drawn to what, on the outside, looked like success; reputation in two cases, an outward appearance of wealth on the other, and an assumption on the other. As I look back, I wouldn't reach out to any of them today. My sources of guidance these days come from folks with experience that I respect and whom I desire to be like. I know them; I feel their energy. They are loving, supportive, and caring. They each lead lives in ways that I want to be. I see how they treat others, I see the quality of their marriages, I feel and hear the wisdom of their insights. They care about me and want me to do well. The quality of guidance I receive is much better and guides me to better decisions, resources, and people to whom I want to be like. I admire their spiritual lives, who they are as people and how they treat others. This is very important. It relates to the issue of *enoughness*. As I come to view myself in a greater sense of *enoughness*, I reach out to, connect with, and ask for help from others who are *enough* in their own right. I feed off and am directed by sources of *enoughness* which guide me to more *enoughness*, more love. But at that time, due to my lack of *enoughness*, I reached out to people who looked like they had it, but in reality were sources of *not enoughness*, because they themselves were caught up in a game of *not enough* with themselves. This is such a powerful element of the addiction to struggle. Even in our attempts to get out of it, we reach out to people and resources that are grounded in *not enough* themselves. We think they must know better, we follow their guidance which leads us more deeply into *not enough* ways of being; struggle.

As Tara and I embarked on creating our new company, *DillonMar-*

cus Executive Retreats, it felt important that I get this stuff right
from the start. Get myself right. Fix what was wrong with me, or
else we'd never succeed. The advice I was about to receive led me
deeper into a place of *not good enough.* The sales coach I went to see
played off of this. His sales process purposefully guided me into my
not enoughness. I felt so uncomfortable. Like the feeling I had in my
interview to Rabbinical School, my instincts were telling me to get
out of here, this is not a good fit for me. But I misread the signs. I
took them as a sign that I must really need this. They have something I need. I'm not good enough so I must need something else;
something *not me.* I took actions based on my insecurity. My way
wasn't working so I couldn't trust myself. I had to become someone else. And I tired really hard; tried to follow the sales system,
to work it right, to become someone I wasn't. I had to because my
way clearly didn't work. Because I was working against my nature;
it was hard. I worked hard at it, but it wasn't genuine to me and
I struggled. I was playing the struggle game really well. I figured
it must be my fault. In my clearer moments, it just didn't feel
right—it felt manipulative. The image I had of a salesman was of
getting someone to buy something. A really good salesman could
get people to buy something they didn't even want. I didn't feel
capable of either. The sales coach had given me an assessment—it
agreed: I didn't have the killer instinct. This is a pattern I lived over
and over. My assessment into Rabbinical School came up short
too. Assessments that told me that I didn't fit in, when in truth, I
don't actually fit in. The problem for me and for many of us is that
we trust these external markers over our internal guidance. What
is so terrific about finding loving people is that they tend to accept
us for who we are. In their presence and in their guidance we feel
better about ourselves, not less than. The more I aspire and lean
into *my enoughness,* the more tuned in I am to who I am with. More
and more I trust sources that lead me into feeling better about me,
more whole, more *good* and I try to steer away from people and
situations that leave me feeling *less than.* The sales assessment determined that my desire for money wasn't great enough. I held too

high a desire to be liked and to help people. I scored very low. But I tried to follow the system; I really tried hard. I struggled a lot. I didn't get any results other than more struggle, despair, and a sense of shame for not being good at something even when I tried really hard at it. This is one of the great travesties of a struggle lifestyle. What happens when you really do struggle hard—hard enough to earn your *good enough points*—and you find out that you aren't good enough, that you can't get the results? Shame. Shame is one of the great payoffs of a struggling life. A terrible price to pay.

Well, I felt the shame of trying hard—really hard—and not getting results. I trusted Bob enough to let him know the truth: The shame I was feeling, how hard I was trying, and the poor results I was getting. I trusted him enough to tell him how frustrated I felt and how scared I was to be struggling financially. Typically, I was afraid to tell people how I was doing financially, that our company was not growing and that we had to borrow money from a family member to get by. The truth was that when I had the courage to tell someone, they didn't treat me with the shame I expected to get back. Most people are respectful and understanding. Still I struggle a bit to share this with people. But, on this day, I shared it with Bob.

Bob laid a whole different story on me. First, he asked me where our business came from. I wasn't sure what he meant. Then he asked, "Doesn't it come out of the blue?" I thought of jobs we had received. Rarely had they come directly from a sales call. Mostly, they were a call *out of the blue*. During my first corporate job—my biggest job—many of our jobs came from out of the blue. I was networking with organizations and only got one direct job from them. So I stopped networking. Eventually jobs stopped coming in. It wasn't until years later that I understood what had happened. I learned that the connection between my activity and the jobs that came in were not necessarily linked. The direct link was between activity and jobs, not a specific activity leading to a specific job. The point to all this is that it was important for me to be active. As one sales guy later described it to me; moving molecules. We need to be out there—meeting people, being with people, being active. The jobs then seem to come from out of the blue. But we can't just sit on our butts. We need to *seed the blue*. Plant seeds in the universe that grow and then come to us; but not always in a linear fashion.

As Bob and I talked about this, it started to hit me that the most important thing I could do was not try and sell people stuff. If the opportunity came out of the blue and I needed to be with people, be active (i.e., *seed the blue*) then it was important to recognize the essence of why I was meeting with people. For me, the easiest reason was quite simple. Help them. Now *that* I could do. I might not be able to get people to buy stuff from me, but if my job was to *seed the blue*, then I certainly could do that. How hard would it be for me to go meet people and try to help them as best as I could? If this reciprocity stuff had any real merit, then I'd be flying great. Reciprocity means what goes around comes around. If I went and helped people in a sincere, genuine, and authentic way, then people would do the same for me. On top of that, the work that would come to me from out of the blue was more likely to come from sincere, genuine, and authentic people. I have found this to be the case. The people we meet and build relationships with trust us because they know we are sincere. Most of the people we work with we have really good relationships with. They know that I'm not trying to pull something over them and they treat me the same. On top of this, as the law of reciprocity continues to work, we get calls from some really great people. Then, by acting sincerely, we don't screw up the gift of a good person. They realize we are for real and, in turn, they act as real as they can with us. I left my first meeting with Bob saying, "So you are telling me that my job is to be a missionary of help?" Then I told him, "How easy is that? I don't believe it will work, but it will be easy." I couldn't believe that something that could come this easily could actually work. I still thought it would have to be hard if it was going to produce results. The funny thing is that I had been trying very hard and still hadn't seen any results. I didn't have much to lose, so I decided to try it.

I don't want this to sound like a fairy tale. Our business did not immediately turn around. There are still months in the year where we are concerned about where the money is going to come from. But what has changed the most is *Us*. Selling, which was my struggle, has turned into one of my favorite things to do. What could be better than going out, meeting people, not expecting to get anything out of them, and having the intention to help them. I don't need anything directly from most of the people I meet with because most of the business will come out of the blue. So I am now free to truly help them the best I can. This is a great job. I have many great meetings with folks. We build a level of respect. We try to help each other.

So this is how I came to drive to an appointment with the intention of helping the person I was going to see. As I continued to let go of my addiction to struggle and began to embrace the *Play* I was writing about, a new intention came to me. Could I simply go on this call with the intention of having fun? Could I simply have fun on the call? Would that be enough? Would that count? Could fun *seed the blue* too? This sounds so easy, but to me it felt radical. This was really letting go. No way could this work. No way could *just* having fun work or produce results in my business. It felt risky. My livelihood was tied to this. I don't get a salary. My money comes from the work we get. Could I trust fun to produce real results (i.e., money)? It felt too easy; too light. The helping people felt right, meaningful, and heavy enough to produce results. Not struggle; but heavy enough. But then I started to think, 'was this just a lighter version of struggle?' The idea was that I needed some heaviness in order to produce results. This applies to everything— from working out, to dieting, to praying, and meditation. Would any of these important things work if I removed all of the heaviness from them? Isn't there some price I need to pay in order to appease the Gods, my body, the financial doings of life? Could just having fun actually produce results other than having fun? Intellectually, I knew the answer. I had seen it work in other areas of my life, but I hadn't tried it on something really important like money, like livelihood, like God stuff, and real health issues. I had tried it on more superficial stuff like rock climbing; but could it work with this too?

I must have tried it once. "Let's just go have some fun." That's it. I even let go of the need to help them. I'm sure I made it into a game for myself. "Okay, we'll try it just this one time. Next time I'll go back to helping people." This type of game always helps me try something new. How much damage could I cause with one time? It's just an experiment. And it really was fun. The conversation flowed and covered all the points. I was freed up. My voice was freed up; both my actual voice and, more importantly, my inner voice; my authentic, genuine truth. As in more open, more openly sharing what I truly thought and felt, more open with my ideas, less afraid of rejection. I can hear and feel the difference when I am free like this. I had a ball. And I'm sure I helped them too. It was great. I bet if you talk to the truly great sales people, they'll tell you that this is what it's about. Forget all that technique stuff—the overcoming objections, and the upsell. All crap. This is truly what it's about. But I still didn't trust. I still don't trust it entirely. Here I am, the proponent of play, and I still get afraid to trust it at times—especially when things seem important: When money feels tight. When it seems like an important appointment. When real issues of health or spirit are on the line. Can I truly trust the play, the fun, and the ease? Can I truly let go of the struggle and get results when it seems like results are really important? Intellectually, I know that under real pressure is when we need to lighten up the most. It's in our play that we free ourselves to do our best work: To free up our intuition, our talent, and our timing. This is when we are most open to coincidence, new ideas, inklings, and chance meetings—when our gifts, our talents, and our passions are unencumbered. We are free to come out and express ourselves. This is when we get energy, perseverance, and courage. This is when our brilliance and our genius really can shine. I know this and yet, at times, I am still afraid to trust it.

Play is enough. It always is. Again, what we are afraid of is that we are not enough.

Play is simple. We just need to let loose. Not just us, but the divine in us. At play, the whole package is set free. But if we don't trust ourselves enough, then letting ourselves loose won't be enough.

If we don't trust the divine, if we don't trust in the basic goodness of life, in our universe, in action, then this won't be enough either. "This is nonsense", we can say intellectually, but that isn't the forum we are dealing with here. We are talking the down and dirty self-assessment.

If we don't think we are enough then no way can we let ourselves out fully when things matter most. Because we won't be enough to handle the situation—and our God isn't enough so she can't handle the situation. So what do we do—what makes up the gap? We rely on the others—the so-called authorities, they must know more. So we give them our power. It could be a spouse, or boss, or guru—or a so-called friend. Or it could be our struggle. The struggle itself will give us more—so we add in struggle.

We need an extra boost to handle the situation we are in. We really do. When we come to believe in a power greater than ourselves, then we have the answer. But here is the key: Have we truly chosen a power greater than ourselves? Have we aligned with a power that can make up the gap? The husband can't do it, not for long; nor can the wife. At our best we have that spiritual awakening—where we connect with a true source that is more powerful than ourselves— a true and loving power that can and will make up the gap—a power that always has been taking up the slack and filling the gap. This is our answer—our answer to the *enough* problem. On our own, we were correct: we are not enough. But there is a power that is—can you find it?

Spiritual journey—this is it, finding our *enoughness*. You may find this higher power is you—literally your own higher power. The spirituality aspect of our being—we need this power side of ourselves. For some, it is God—another source outside of us that gives us power and love. Maybe it's an amalgam. A loving power that is both other and fully us—we of it, it of us. Maybe your higher power is a rock or a tree, or a whole committee of deities. The spectrum is open wide, open to what this higher divine power is. But in our take, and that of many others, this is our only real answer to the *enough/not enough* question.

God is not enough. Why is that? Because it is our conceptions of God that are not enough. I remember early on, believing that I could create God—one that would work for me—not as a job, but the concept that God would get me excited; give me enthusiasm and excitement to go out into life with more hope, trust, and enthusiasm. That God would get me excited about my life and your life. Now if you could create and believe in this God, then this God would be enough. But the one you have right now might not be enough. So we can get pissed off and go and find something else, or we can do our job and create a bigger, better, cooler, God—one that is more than enough.

3.8 A Case for Enoughness

As soon as we switch our attention and start to grow evidence of *the enough, of the plenty,* then we begin to break the grasp of the struggle. This is why making gratitude lists and developing gratitude are so powerful. In these moments, we are building a case for *enoughness.* In this enough, we get all the benefits that she brings—feelings of gratitude, more peace, a greater sense of well-being, and more room to play. Here is the real kicker. As we focus on having enough, it gives us more energy, and better solutions to tackle the areas of our lives that aren't enough. The clothes don't magically hop into the drawer, but we sure will have more energy to put them away. As we put them away, we break down the struggle again. As long as we let them sit there, we get mad, and become paralyzed to actually do anything about it. As we take action, especially in a space of gratitude; we feel better. We feel better for taking the action. We feel better for living in the solution and we feel better because the place is no longer such a mess. This too energizes us and now we are *on a roll of enoughness*, building momentum, going with the *gravity of plenty*. The enoughness too needs food, and we can feed it by seeing in enough, acting in enough, being grateful for enough, seeing ourselves, seeing the divine as enough, seeing others as enough—having a whole smorgasbord of enoughness.

3.9 No Strain

I was working out this morning with a stick. Over the past year I got into making walking sticks; I give them away to people who want and appreciate them. But this one is for me. It's about 5 feet long. We were watching *The Karate Kid* and one of the scenes at the temple shows a guy using a stick in his King Fu movements. It looked really cool; the kind of movements I like to do. So I started playing around with my stick. Moving it in all kinds of directions; my body too then began to move. Then I started to play a game that I often play: the *no strain gain*. See, as I moved with the stick, I found myself in moments of strain, depending how deeply I extended my legs or stretched out my arms. This is not the kind of strain that would cause me to yell. It is a subtle strain. But the addiction to struggle tells me that I need this kind of strain to get any kind of gain. Again, this is a belief that I like to play with. What if this is just not true? So I decide to engage in movements that are simply easy, with no strain. In one way, this limits the extension and fullness of the movements I will choose because I keep my movements limited to those that are easy and comfortable. Again, the **Addicted to Struggle** thinking process tells me that this may feel good, may be fun, but in no way will it do anything to promote my strength, endurance, posture, or well-being. Without the strain, there can be no gain. What could possibly grow? Again, this is nonsense. As I continue my movements that flow effortlessly, in the subtle foundation of my body, my muscles, tendons, and blood starts to flow, warmth is spreading, and my subtle body is awakening and becoming more alive, limber, and engaged. Without me really feeling it, my movements start to grow, through ease. The ease continues, and subtly my pace picks up naturally, my movements naturally expand, but the ease stays the same. The growth is happening and my ease is expanding. No struggle, no pain. There is subtle, expanding, and enjoyable gain.

This is always the promise of play. A promise that allows us the opportunity to grow, to expand, to increase, to deepen in joy, in ease, in brilliance, with a smile on our face, rejuvenated, our bodies and minds nourished—and no broken bones. It takes less time to do, but I end up spending more time, because there is less resistance. Knowing that I'm about to do one push up, or engage in enjoyable movements with a stick, my mind and my body have less to resist. As I build my belief that the ease is brilliance, again I am taking away some of the struggle arsenal—and there is less resistance. What is there to avoid? Why would I procrastinate from the enjoyable? As long as I am building a belief system that sees the struggle for what it truly is—a hollow promise of filling up my feeling of not good enough—and as long as we continue to build up our belief in the power, value, impact, and meaning of ease, play, and joy; then we will continue to lower our thresholds of entry. We will release the need for resistance and we will build a strong easy desire and willingness to participate. We will increase our enthusiasm, our natural desire, our joy; and thus we will start throwing ourselves into our activities with a calm, peaceful gusto. Not only are we now participating, we are also participating with the energy of a master, a craftsmen; paying attention to detail, conducting our activities with passion, commitment, attention, presence. We are getting into the nooks and crannies; doing really good, deep work. Cleaning in the corners—and feeling a sense of pride for our accomplishment. No longer do we have to rush through it, muscle our way, or knock stuff out of the way as we do our best to get this chore done. Behaving in this manner can transform your exercising, cleaning, sales calls, or projects into an act of love and art, craftsmanship, and beauty. All because we dropped the strain and embraced the ease.

> "... it seems illogical to them that there is power in relaxation, in letting go, or in love or joy or bliss. Most people do not understand that their true power lies in releasing resistance—which is the only obstacle to their true power."

> "Most people do not expect their path to great abundance to be one of ease and of joy. They have been taught that struggle and hardship and sacrifice are requirements that must be met before the reward of great abundance can be realized. Most do not understand that the very struggle they deliberately involve themselves in, in their quest for success and advantage, actually works against them."

> *Abraham Hicks—daily quotes—September 25, 2011*

3.10 Why I Work

If all is well, then what is the purpose of my work? Am I working for money? Am I trying to get what I want? Do I have to manipulate something to get what I need? Are we growing a business, increasing market share? Why are we working? What is our purpose? How do we apply our spiritual values, our higher selves, and our ease to work? If I don't have to find personal approval at work; if I'm not looking for my enoughness through my work, if we don't have to struggle at work, if we release our work from the struggle game, then why do we work?

Why would you want to work? What are the reasons that would be uplifting and inspiring to you? What would help you feel better about yourself and your purpose? What purpose would make your work easier, more inspiring, and uplifting? You may not have to change what you are doing but rather shift your purpose. Why are you there and doing your thing? We can shift our desires, our purpose, our way of working, of seeing what we are doing, and why we are doing it. This is playing within our purpose.

Is our real work this work of clarity—of becoming clear of our purpose? What is our purpose? Why are we here? How do we realize that purpose that is enlivening, meaningful, and uplifting to us and the people around us? We can desire to be pumped and enthusiastic at work and we just may be able to do this, but imagine what we are capable of when we truly align ourselves with our highest purposes; when we are clear about our passion, our desires, and we all work together towards reaching them. The power and energy, the enthusiasm unleashed is incredible. The word *work* itself transforms. It is no longer a tool of burden and struggle because we transform our work into an outlet of our creativity, our power, and our talents. It becomes a game in the most sacred space. We are unleashed, like an avalanche. This is a great idea, one that is hard, maybe impossible, to achieve if we are not authentically connected to our purpose. Again, this may not require a change in your job, but rather your perception of what your job really is, and the way you go about doing that job. If you try to find and prove your enoughness through your work, then it will be a losing battle—you are now thrown into the game of struggle.

But once you find that your enoughness does not come from your struggle, then why work, why be a parent, why work out, or volunteer? If we are enough, if we are already whole and complete, then why live? What is our purpose here on this planet, in our offices, in our homes, in our families, on the basketball court? What gives our lives meaning?

For me, the spiritual life is made up of many aspects. At the core, it is about learning and coming to have a deeper relationship with God. In the learning mode, I have the opportunity to learn more about myself—my motivations, my purpose, who I am, what drives me, who I have been, why I am the way that I am. I also get to learn about others. From this learning comes the development of spirituality principles—like compassion, commitment, persistence, and love. The learning about self is not just for the sake of it. There has to be action behind this. How do I become a more compassionate, persistent, and loving person? This has to be the outcome. The knowledge and awareness are steps along the way, but it's the action, the new action, that is the goal. And this is the healing aspect of our lives. Every situation that I am in gives me the chance to learn, to take new action, and to find healing for myself and others. I have opportunities to change old behavior patterns; to let go of the old and to embrace the new. To be of service to myself and to others. To help others on their path of learning, action, and healing. So this is my purpose. Why I go to work. Why I have a family. Why I play golf. Don't let the outer purpose divert us. I may be hitting golf balls and enjoying myself, but the real game is the game of healing; coming to know myself. To help others and to develop a relationship with God, or higher power, or however you define this life force. For me, it has been a journey of a personal relationship— of coming to talk to, and rely on, and live with God. My conception of God has changed and is changing all the time. Work is an incredibly fertile ground for this exploration, this development of self, of my relationship to God, and my understanding of my purpose. It is a process of learning and development itself—one of developing clarity—over time. So why do we work? It's a great place to let go of our struggle, to embrace our love, to learn about ourselves, to develop spirituality, to be of service to others, and to continue on our journey of developing a relationship with spirit. It is also a terrific place to struggle if you choose to. It's fun. Isn't that enough?

When I come home from work, I want to come home enthused, inspired, and excited to talk about my work. If I'm tired, it is the *good tired* of being engaged in my efforts and my creativity. When I think of work I want to think about possibility; about impact. I want to be enthusiastic, grateful, and looking forward to what may happen. Who can we help? What might we learn? I want my work to be a source of joy and meaning.

If all is well, then what would you do right now?

Work is Fun!

I am having a blast.

I love my job.

It's a lot of fun.

I love playing around and trying new stuff.

I can't wait to get to work.

3.11 The Internal Flame

In synagogues all around the world, you will find an *eternal* flame glowing. Most of these are powered electrically but they symbolize the commitment to keep the flame of worship alive at all times. This goes back to when the temple of Jerusalem was central to the worship of Judaism. There are many traditions of eternal flames. In play, I too am looking for such a source—in this case an *internal* flame. How do I keep my internal flame alive, glowing, and robust? It is a drag when our flame is low, or barely flickering. Life feels so much better when we are alive, full of life, engaged, enthusiastic, and motivated—when the internal flame is burning brightly. I often relegate the condition of this flame to circumstance. It just seemed to be that way. The flame could be up or down, but I didn't realize my role in this game. I thought it was governed by external affairs or luck or coincidence—like the weather. But our knowledge about play teaches us that we have a much greater control on the lever determining the size and quality of our inner flame than we realize.

3.12 Watch it Grow

Many of us are out there planting seeds, fertilizing, and watering. Isn't it fun to go outside each day to see what has come up? Well, let's imagine that the stuff we pay attention to is the stuff that grows. This is why it is important to know what brings us joy and satisfaction. Because the more we are aware of it, the better chance we have of choosing it, doing it, and thus experiencing more joy and satisfaction. Why leave it up to chance? It gets even better. The more we pay attention to something, the more it seems to just happen to us. Today's game is easy. Just pay attention to the things you enjoy; notice what you like, who inspires you, and what is fun. You don't have to DO anything, just watch. By the way, if you keep watching, it will start growing all by itself. Ummm, how nice is that? Here NOW.

3.13 Holy Work

What does it mean to do holy work? My first thoughts are images of helping lepers, living like a hermit, or crafting religious ceremonial objects out of silver. I imagine quiet, subdued, alone, white robes, chanting, living in a remote place, and helping the *less fortunate*. These images feel heavy and limited. At the same time, I'm interested in turning my work, our daily work, into holy work—Work that is divinely inspired and purposed. Work that is alive, ripe and dripping with Godly ooze. Work that is passionate and contributes to the fulfillment of life's potential. Wearing white robes and sandals and living in the desert can't be the only way to do this. How do we do it right now, with the clothes we are wearing, in the houses we are living in, and in the offices and businesses where we currently work? How do we do holy work with a whistle, a smile, and a lightness of being— in our cars, in front of our sinks, while working with our customers? This is the playground of holy work that inspires me. There is great potential here to transform our lives—here in the everyday, right here, right now. I love this idea—it inspires me. Now, how do we go about doing it? This is what I'm drawn to and what I have decided to explore—transforming the everyday into the holy. Let's go see what is holy for you and for me….

At first, I got caught up in THE holy work as if it is one thing that I need to learn to do. Now I am reminded that this too is an explanation; a game. Not so much in doing it right but in starting to learn what holy work means to me. What does it mean for me to do holy work at this point in my life? This is much more engaging: The experiment, the discovery, the exploration. What can I learn about holy work? What can I learn about what makes this work? Where is the line between holy vs. not holy? I once saw an interview with Martha Graham. She was just walking on stage. She started talking to the audience. Her exploration or discovery was trying to understand when this thing called walking turned into dance. At what point does walking turn into dance? What is the moment? What is the transformative element that turns one thing into another— what does it? What trips it? What changes it? What is it that changes work into holy work? Do you know what it is for you? Come with me on my journey. I'll share with you what I'm finding. In one year, or five, or ten: It may be really different than it is now—or maybe not. But why not start now? Here we go.

What would make this writing holy? When does it transform into the holy like Graham's walking? Let's see. I just stopped to take a breath. I closed my eyes, breathed in, stopped. My purpose is to connect to divine; to connect to my highest intelligence. To let go and allow these ideas to flow. The breath is an act of reminding myself what I am to do. To tap into my source of intelligence, to let go and allow the ideas to flow. The breath, the stopping, the continuing to the divine. I remember why I am writing this. Not for myself, not for my own aggrandizement, but as a way to help others, to serve. To let go again of why I am writing this, to let it out, to be of service. What else makes it holy? Taking my time, in a way. I'm actually writing as fast as I can type, but I'm not rushing as much. The holy attitude reminds me that I can't screw this up. It doesn't have to be perfect; the perfection will come out naturally. I can go fast, not rushing, because rushing is part of my ego. I've got to get it right. I feel rushed as I try to get it all out. When I'm taking a holy approach I know that I am not alone, I feel less alone. It's not just me doing it. It's okay to take my time. This only means that I want to savor and enjoy. This can be an enjoyable and meaningful act. So it is okay to take my time. Even going fast is enjoyable, without the rush, without the nervousness of going fast. I'm still feeling a bit of tightness in my chest. Is this because of the act of writing or because of what I'm writing? I'm still feeling some pressure to get it right but less than may be normal. I'm feeling pressure; pressure around money, about the state of our business, about the nature of the day. How can I use this writing to help me with what I am feeling? With who I am, what I need to do, with tapping into resources, and asking for help? What makes writing holy? Am I concerned about what you think of me, of how my writing will be received, of that which takes me away from holy? This holy thing is probably not a yes or a no. I'm sure it has to do with a continuum of holy. I can lean toward the holy side of this service and be aware that a spirit is working with me, through me, or I can lean toward the profane in my ego—it's my writing, it's about my reputation. What else makes it holy work? Me. I can ask God to help me. I can see it as prayer, a form of giving thanks, or asking for help. I can see it as an act of learning, learning about myself, learning more about spirituality, using this writing as a way to build a relationship with myself, a relationship with God; getting to know each other. It's slowing down. It can lean towards an act of meditation. I can stop. Breath again.God helps me use this writing to express ideas to help others be who they can: Lets me be a source of healing and freedom.

I was planting some flowers last week. I was bending over, digging with a shovel, when I felt some discomfort in my body. I stopped a moment and made a decision to turn it into holy work. I asked myself, what would make this holy? The first ingredient was my body. I tried to reposition my body to put it more at ease, to more fully engage myself in the activity. I also did this while putting screws in a bracket. I moved and repositioned my body to make it as easy as possible to get fully involved in the movement without the contorted stretching. I've learned that, when I do this, I actually become closer to the activity itself. I have literally put more of my body into it. Bending myself deeper, moving my torso closer to the shovel, the group, or the bracket. It feels like a yoga position. The yoga of putting this screw into this bracket, or digging this hole with this shovel; moving my body to be more into it. I like this game. It's fun for me to find a better body position, one that is more at ease and into the action, more supported. When screwing the bracket, I ended up laying down on my back, underneath the table, reaching up rather than bending over and reaching far in. It was a much better position. What makes this holy? I'm not sure, but to me it feels more holy when I put more of myself into it. Caring for my body in how I am using myself; the intentionality of it. The use of my body, the exploration of finding a body position. It's not just about the screw, it's about finding ease, about putting myself more into something. What is my mind thinking about while I'm doing something? Am I distracted? The distraction of thinking about the discomfort takes me more toward the side of the unholy. Being more present, my mind's attention on the activity is what is leaning more toward the holy. This is part of what I am finding out.

I was washing dishes. I decided that this a holy activity.

3.14 Preparing for a Training Presentation

I'm not very excited about this one. I'm not happy with the people we are working for and how they have treated us. We've already been paid and I don't want to work for or with them again. So how do I make this holy work? First, I start off with that decision to choose to make this holy work. Then I shut my eyes and take a breath. This is not a set ritual. I hadn't planned on the routine of shutting my eyes and taking a breath. It's what I naturally did. I can play with this. Maybe I didn't have to shut my eyes and take a breath to mark the beginning of a *holy act* but, for right now, that is what I did. God help me take this on with love and respect for you, for myself and for these people. How can I be helpful today? Who can I help? In what ways can I be helpful? Who can I love? Who may need my love and care today? Maybe not the principals of the session: It might be the toll taker, the receptionist, or Tara. I may not be aware of who the person is. Let's be open to being helpful; maybe even upbeat and positive. There is some reason I am going there today. Let me be the person I love to be. Let me prepare and do my best work, or at least very good work. Not for them, but for me so that I can feel proud of myself and good about my work regardless of how I feel about them. Let me be clean in my interaction; kind and positive to all that I meet. Let me not get caught up in resentment or anger so I can prepare again, read over, and practice the material. I need to look good, prepare myself well, and be open to helping folks. Be open to the people I meet and do my best. I certainly can be kind and helpful to Tara; to love her. I can make it even holier by remembering that I am here for a purpose: to do God's work and be a blessing to others. That part is fun for me. I never know who I'm going to meet. I may have an awareness at some point and I realize that is why I am here. Or I will learn a new lesson about myself or about life. Or some issue in my life will continue to get healed during this process. All of this contributes to my sense of the holy nature of my life. Maybe that is part of it. The more I am aware or choose to believe that the mere nature of my life is holy, that life itself is holy, then anything I am doing is in the context of holiness. As in, I shouldn't do anything to make it less holy. The question is being aware and treating the holy as holy. So today, maybe the most holy I can manage is to have fun. To have fun today, can I accept that as holy? Can I accept that having fun and playing with today is an act of *holy-fying the holy*? Now that would be cool.

The truth is that this kind of play and fun we are talking about is not making light of or being less respectful of people or the work. This kind of play is finding ways to throw myself fully into my work, to be present, to be alive and attentive; to be fully engaged, passionate, aware, and creative. To bring my spontaneity, to be able to react in the moment, to follow the script with energy. That's the kind of play, of inviting others in, playing with them, helping them to be more playful, to have fun, to get it, and to get excited. That's pretty good stuff. Can I see that as holy? The old model wants me on my hands and immersed in quiet, solemn, serious stuff. Not bad, but can I liberate my mind and my understanding of the sacred to embrace the play as holy. So let's go out today and see how much fun we can have. Let's see what happens. An experiment in play, excellence, and holy. I'll report back.

3.15 Cola / Uncola

I can still remember those commercials for 7-Up. It featured someone choosing between a cola and an Uncola—something different from the ordinary cola. Something special, something clean—the drink itself is not a murky color: it was clear, it was clean, it was see-though, it was supposed to be light, more effervescent, uncluttered, alive, free, carbonated and bubbly—ahhh the Uncola.

> 'No caffeine, no artificial color, no artificial flavor, clean, refreshing, unspoiled taste, light and refreshing, and crisp and clean. A clean, crisp change from the every day—7-Up, the Uncola. It's marvelous...don't you feel good about 7-Up? Put some Un in your life.'

Our world of struggle and un-struggle is very similar. We have a voice. It's not the situation itself; it's how we react to, live in, and orient ourselves within the situation. It amazes me how simple and profound this is. It shows up not only in the existential sense of life, but also in a very simple way. How I drive somewhere, how I make sales calls, how I handle a cavity. All of it is grounds for struggle and grounds for un-struggle; for peace and for ease. We constantly have this choice in action. It can be on a life scale as we shift from a struggle life to one of love, but the playground for this is real life. It's not just in the ether of life.

The struggle and the peace have to live, to eat, and to love. They need a place in our lives and it is happening in every moment, in every situation we're in. We have a choice: To give the struggle a place to live and breathe or give the ease, peace, and love a place to live and breathe. Both need food and fodder, a tangible expression of themselves. This can be awesome and it can be a curse. The awesomeness is the every day ease of the situation where we get to make these decisions all day long. We get to practice it and live it out. It doesn't have to be some big, philosophical, untouchable issue; it's very tangible. The curse is that until we face and realize it, the struggle will get to live itself out all day, in all of our every day, little decisions—from how we drive somewhere to handling a broken freezer. We can't escape it. The situations will present themselves to us all day; every day. We can't run away from it, even when we're on vacation. Our struggle strategy will follow us to church, to Hawaii, and even to the psychiatrist's office. It comes with us everywhere we are breathing. We can't run from it. The same goes with the promise of freedom. We get to play it out all the time—in every situation we face. We get a chance to get traction, to build up our capacity, to get the momentum and ball rolling on our side, on the side of freedom, of peace of mind, of ease, of faith and hope, and of un-struggle. Let's explore it. Let's look at these everyday opportunities to play the struggle or the un-struggle game.

Situation

Our freezer is not working properly. The ice cube maker is not working. Stuff is soft.

Struggle

'Damn it. Where is the money coming from to fix this? It's going to cost a fortune. We can't afford a new refrigerator. Look how much money we've already spent.'

I feel frustrated. A bit defeated. Mad.

I sit on it. Worry about it. Think about calling Otto, the repair guy. Ruminate about the bigness of the situation, the problems, how it won't work out, and the distress it will cause us. I keep trying to make the freezer not be broken. I close the door hard and don't open it for two days to see if I can make it work.
—Un Struggle.

After I make sure the door is shut and leave it closed overnight, everything is still not cold.

So I call Otto—no drama, I just make the call and shut down the worry voice. I tell myself it will work out—the main thing is to take action easily, remove the drama and just do it. I tell myself it will work out whatever it is. I visualize it working and imagine telling someone the story and what an easy solution there was—'he didn't even charge us.' I visualize positive results.

I called on Monday morning. They sent a guy out Monday afternoon. He tweaked a few things and just charged us for a service call—$92.50. That evening when I checked, it wasn't any cooler. I want to get worried again; I start imagining having to buy a new $4,000 refrigerator to replace this one, and all the work it will take. I shut down my thinking and decide I will call him again in the morning. Take it one step at a time. Struggle and Un-struggle.

The End: We bought a new refrigerator. We needed to finance it since we didn't have the cash; took us about 2 years to pay it off. I was worried about getting rid of the old one. It was a SubZero built in and one salesman told me it would require a separate crew to take it out and then an electrician to rewire my outlet. Worrying about this kept us from buying a new one in the first place—Struggle. Once we let go of the struggle and purchased the new one, the whole process got easier. The guys we bought it from just came out, took the old one and installed the new one. No big deal, no extra charge.

3.16 Mechanics of Misery

I know people who live in misery. I live there too. When I am, it felt as if someone in the world had a voodoo doll that looked like me. And they pricked it and I felt the pain. They pricked it a lot. I felt in pain a lot of the time. I tried to make it go away—therapy, masturbation, meditation, journaling, praying, medicine, boxing, sex—I tried, but it didn't go away. At times it got worse. But it didn't feel like my fault. It was happening to me. I couldn't see the role I was playing—how I was creating my own misery. I can see when it's happening with other people; in the actions they take, their mindset, belief systems, sense of right and wrong, and how they do things. I watch it in the choices people make, in how they confront and engage with life's situations. How they eat, what they eat, the language they choose to use, what they talk about, and who they talk to. It's evident in our patterns, how we were raised, in literally who we have become, the constellation of our make-up, how we operate on a day-to-day basis, how we pray, what we buy—our motivations and intentions that underlie each and every activity we engage in, and every thought we have. It's buried here, both deep and on the surface of the quality of our lives; this is where the mechanics of misery lie. Not on the end of some voodoo needle, or in our fate, or in how God created us.

3.17 Love, Faith, and Work

We've allowed ourselves to be conditioned to believe that words like productivity, efficiency, and profitability are our primary business objectives. But what if, we decided to direct our primary business focus at love and faith. As we pursue our spiritual path to enoughness, our business lives are a ripe platform to discover and to practice our spiritual lives. So much of our lives are played out in our work; so too our addiction to struggle. The good news is that our work offers us a terrific and powerful opportunity, every day, to foster love, peace of mind, and faith to move away from our struggle.

3.18 My Blankie

Where do we get our protection from? As adults, where do we get our sense of protection? Do I need to struggle in order to feel protected? If I am afraid to be forced, then where else can I get a sense of my protection? How do I feel and stay aware that I am protected, cared for, watched over, and safe?

My first reaction is simple: protection comes from God. It comes from a working relationship, a direct relationship, a one-on-one relationship with a higher power; a loving force in my life. It comes from somehow knowing that I am good enough. How do I come to know that? What if I am good enough simply because I was born? The fact that I was born into life is all the proof that we need that we are good enough. As I friend of mine used to say, "God doesn't create crap." If we were created by a divine force, then why would that divine force create anything other than perfection? You or me, or the person you desire may not look perfect in this world; or certain conditions in life may not look perfect, but what if it is? Not just perfect as a human would define it, but perfection that is divine perfection? Our job on this planet, in this life form, could be coming to understand and get glimpses of this perfection. Just because I don't understand it doesn't mean that it doesn't exist. What if we assumed that we were complete, whole, or good enough, simply because we were breathing; simply because we were born into being. Maybe that is all the proof that we need. But even if I'm aware of this, intellectually, how do I come to believe it? How do I come to know, believe, be aware of, and really understand that I am, that you are, that we are, good enough? Is this the purpose of our spiritual path, of our spirituality at work—to come to understand our *enoughness*? I can relate to a life purpose that is about having a relationship with a higher power. That makes sense to me. But could part of that journey be a relationship with my higher power? Not one that is separate from me, like a friend, but my higher power; my *enoughness*? Could my higher power be me? In this case, my journey of *enoughness* is itself my spiritual journey. It's not getting the seal of approval from another; even if that other is God. That still sets us up to look for an outer source to give us our *enoughness*. But what if that *enoughness* comes from me—myself? What if I believe that I am, my divine self, my higher power? My *enoughness* is not a static thing, like a goal line that I cross. That *enoughness* itself could be abundant—a constant and continual journey of discovery. Imagine that *enoughness* was a gold mine. An unending gold mine, one that could not be depleted—

ever. Could my, your, our, *enoughness* be a tangible force? We are always enough and, at the same time, are continually coming into discovery and building a relationship with our *enoughness*. Now the problem with this is that it would imply that I am going toward that *enoughness*; that there is part of me—now—that isn't enough. Would it ever go away? How do I pursue more, a deeper understanding of *enoughness*, and still feel enough? Do I do so without the sense of not *enoughness*? Is that even possible or must we accept that, as humans, in this form of life, that there will be a part of ourselves that never is enough. That our human form itself is an incomplete form—that we simply aren't enough in this form—and that the *enoughness* is something we strive for, collect and build, learn about, taste, and share with others. I can take solace in knowing that when I transition from this form to a more complete form, then I will experience my *enoughness*. Another take on this is that we are enough, our form is perfect, complete, and whole. Forget this original sin—that Adam and Eve did something wrong. What if that too is some bullshit that we've been subjected to? What if that was an example of not *enoughness*? An incomplete version of who we are. What if we are enough, whole and complete, in this form? How do we come to understand this, to experience, to gain the freedom of mind, of spirit, of understanding, of health, of joy, and of vitality on a physical, mental, and spiritual level? To gain a freedom so that we don't need to struggle, to feel less than, to experience the sabotaging need to carry the security blanket of pain and suffering? How do we get our freedom? How do we come to know that we are truly enough? How do I come to accept life on life's terms without the need to augment it in order to feel safe? How do we do that?

3.19 Enough

It seems that taking life one day at a time is a good place to start. It comes in accepting the spiritual nature of our life—it comes in our meditation , our prayer, and our coming to see ourselves as spiritual beings. It seems to come as we hop on the train of pursuing and cultivating spiritual life. Could it be that simple? That it isn't the proverbial event, but a coming to believe in, cultivate, and practice a spiritual life. Each one of us finding a path, a source, a power greater than ourselves—not just a being that is greater, but a path, a process, a relationship, an ongoing discovery, participation, exploration, trying to find a base and then continuing to develop a power greater than ourselves. Could this process itself be enough—divine in itself? Could this process of discovery, our spiritual journey, itself be divine—not a journey into or toward the divine? Our life is not some preparation for heaven, for completion, but this journey—our life itself—is divine, whole, complete, and enough. This is enough, not a striving for enough, but enough in itself. What if this is what we are here to figure out? We are enough, we are enough, we simply are enough. There is no other option—no *not-enoughness*, we are already enough, we are enough, we are enough.

> *We are enough,*
> *I am enough,*
> *you are enough,*
> *she is enough,*
> *even that asshole is enough,*
> *they are enough.*
> *Ahh, hhh—relief. Enough!*

3.20 Biz Lingo

Where is there room for words like kindness, fairness, love, and caring in the liturgy of the business vernacular? Not just when we are talking about raising money, or doing charitable work, but right at the center of it all. When the money matters? When the deal is being made? When it is time to make the big decisions that matter? Are we willing to take these principles seriously? Yes, we have to if we are going to incorporate spirituality into business. This stuff has to be front and center when the shit really matters because this is not just nice stuff to have; this is the core of how we do things, where our power lies, and where our greatest strength and allies are. So when something matters we need to bring out the big artillery, the spiritualty stuff. This is where it belongs. This is where it takes courage to trust the purity when what's important is on the line. For many, this will sound absurd because they have already made that kind of commitment. The evidence has proven itself to them. There is no other choice but to rely on the spirit at all times. They know this is their greatest strength—and what to rely on when the going gets real. They have taken the risk and used courage to try this when it really mattered. They have the evidence. It may still be challenging, really challenging, and tempting to get dishonest, controlling, and closed-minded. That is still our tendency, and we've been raised and trained to live this way. This is its greatest hour, when the fear is brimming. This is the time to put faith and courage and honesty and patience to the test. When something big is on the line. So move over; its time has arrived. We'd like to welcome love, faith, and caring to the boardroom.

3.21 Working My Ass Off

I'm sitting at dinner and I'm over-hearing a young man trying to explain to his dad why he is leaving his job. He says to his dad, "I've been working my ass off." This is his justification for leaving. He hasn't received the props from his CEO or made the progress he wanted. Maybe he didn't perform to his boss' expectations but at least he worked his ass off. To him, this is more important than actual results. This is a huge problem. People are more interested is using sweat as an indication of a job well done rather than actually performing a job well done. Most jobs can be done really well and effectively in a state of engagement without a lot of hard work. But we don't respect work done in ease. We'll make it hard because that is what we believe is rewarded by our bosses, customers, and God herself. We even con ourselves into believing it is a just reward. Let's start honoring two things. One: Results. The actual results that move things forward and make a difference. Two: Genius work done using our gifts—be it 5 minutes or 10 hours a week.

Let's honor work done with grace, elegance, and smarts. Work done with ease and an efficient use of energy, magic, good luck, and intuition. Let's honor the chance meetings that lead to great things. Let's honor the gifts from God and good karma; the reciprocity that comes from good people doing good things; people who don't work their asses off and still have plenty of energy for friendship, parenting, beautiful hobbies, fun, and free time. This sounds pretty honorable to me.

I trust myself, I trust myself entirely, I am strong, I am beautiful, I am full of knowledge. I know what to do, I know how to heal.

I am full of life, I am full of vigor, I am vibrant, I am wonderful, I am full of life.

Life is coursing through my veins, though my body, through my mind. I am life, I am strong, vibrant, powerful. I am full of life.

My body is brilliant, My body knows what to do. I am confident, I am clear, I am crystal clear, It's ok to be confident, It's ok to be clear.

I am full of grace. I am blessed, blessings are coming my way all day long, I love being blessed, I love being care more.

Magic is all around me.

Everything I need is given to me, easily.

I live with trust, and faith.

I trust you, I trust me. I trust everything that is happening to me.

I am wonderful.

I am a blessed child.

I am loved, I am thoroughly loved.

My mother loves me,

My father loves me,

God loves me.

I love me.

I am the child of a happy God.

I am a happy child of a happy God.

I am the child of a loving God.

I am a loving child of a loving God.

I am alive in love,

Love is all there is.

I am safe,

My life is safe.

Safety is all there is.

I am alive,

I love being alive.

I am thrilled. I am at peace.

I am happy,

Today is a ball.

All kinds of good stuff are happening to me.

My hopes and dreams are real.

I can trust my dreams.

I trust myself.

I trust myself today.

Today is really a blast. I love being alive today.

All kinds of great stuff are happening today.

I love being alive.

I love being alive today.

Today is a great day to be alive.

I am happy.

I smile all day long.

I am peaceful.

I am thrilled to be alive.

My body is brilliant.

My body is absolutely brilliant.

I can really trust her.

She is alive, healing, and brilliant.

I can trust her. She knows what to do.

She knows what she is doing.

Everything I feel is alive, is peace, is growth, is power.

I am powerful.

My body is really powerful.

My body is really beautiful.

My body is really cool.

My body is really kind to me.

My body knows exactly what to do.

My body really loves me.

I trust my body.

I trust myself.

I trust my life.

I am strong.

I am beautiful.

I am confident.

My body is my friend.

My body cares for me.

My body is really great.

My body loves me.

I love my body.

I am strong,

I am healthy,

I am alive!

I am free.

I am totally free.

I am free to enjoy my life.

I am free to travel.

I am free to be rich.

I am free to be confident.

I am free to try.

I am free to succeed.

I am free to be happy.

I am free to be content.

I am free to be peaceful.

I am free to roam.

I am free to write a great book.

I am free to enjoy my children.

I am free to live with hope.

I am free to feel confident.

I am free to have fun.

I am free to thrive.

I am free to be really successful.

I am free to receive great gifts.

I am free to think great thoughts.

I am free to sleep.

I am free to have fun.

I am free.

I am free to make mistakes.

I am free to screw up.

I am free to say the wrong thing.

I am free to break stuff.

I am free to forget.

I am free to lose my keys.

I am free!

I am whole and complete,

Just as I am,

Right now, right here,

I am whole and complete.

I am fun to be with.

People trust me a lot.

I have a lot to offer.

I am very attractive.

People count on me.

I help many people.

I am full of knowledge.

I know what to do.

I am brilliant.

3.22 Affirmations of Un-Struggle

We can use affirmations and self-talk to help recalibrate our thinking, our consciousness, and the way we self-program our lives. Bob once told me that we need to train our brains to be our best friends. I love this. I also know that my thinking is my breeding ground for struggle. Here are some of the affirmations I use to help foster, create, and engrain struggle in my life. Some of them come in the form of a question. It's bad enough to have these thoughts, but as I buy into them they gain momentum, they feel real; and each time I repeat and believe them, they become more engrained—a bad habit. They start to dictate my self-image, they guide my actions, they create feelings and sensations in my body. I literally become their prisoner.

Here are some of my affirmations of struggle.

Is our business failing?

Where is our money coming from?

What will happen to our children? Will they be safe?

Work is too much to handle.

Success will be too hard.

I don't like how I feel.

I feel insecure.

I am weak.

I am unsure.

I don't think I can handle this.

This is too much for me.

I don't have what they have.

He is way smarter than me.

I will never get better.

I feel very alone.

I'm not sure what to do.

I should be better than I am.

We should have more money.

This book will never fly. It will never sell.

We will always be mediocre.

We will never really succeed.

We are stuck.

This is too hard.

We are stuck.

BTW, one of the ways I create affirmations is to take these *natural* struggle messages and turn them on their head. I use them to create their opposite. Instead of *We are Stuck*, I can create: *We are in the Flow of Something Great*. Instead of, *This is Too Hard*, I can create: *Our Success is Easy*. You get the idea. Go ahead and try it for yourself.

3.23 Rubber Meets the Road

Our whole life, all of it—work, sex, health, relationships, money—all of it is a playing field for the spirit. In this field we practice our spirituality, discover it, use it, put it into play; 24/7. There is no place, no time, no aspect of life that is outside the bounds of the spirit. Every area of our life is impacted by spirit and there is no area of our life that doesn't improve by our bringing our spirit to it. Heck it's already there. What we bring is our intention, our attention, our will, our desire, our work, our commitment to spirit; to align ourselves with what is already there. This is where the magic lies. For me it isn't a burst of magic that illuminates and rectifies every issue in my life. It is a slow continual life-long process. I'm not sure what the magic is at times. In the moment it's hard for me to see it. Sometimes it's crystal clear in the moment but generally for me, it's in the overall pattern of my life. It's in refection that I can see the changes, the impact the evidence of spirit working in my life. It has taken me time to come to a point where I see the need and desire to align every aspect of my life with spirit, with wisdom, with God. It is a continual process of learning more and more how and when to surrender, to accept, to give over, and to receive more and more of my life in consort with God; with spirit. I am very grateful to have developed and to be developing this all-encompassing relationship. It gives me so much peace to realize that it's all in the realm of spirit; all of life, all of my life. It gives me so much more peace to accept and receive spirit, to receive energy, and to receive knowledge in all areas. It is a terrific accomplishment that I can turn to *God spirit* for all of my needs—For all of my needs.

The issue of spirituality in business has become quite natural. *Bossiness* like all other areas of my life falls under the same power, the same divine process as everything else. It just makes sense to me, seems very logical. If I truly care about my business, why wouldn't I align it with the most powerful life forces of the universe; with life itself. It's a no brainer—Almost dumb to do anything else. Why work against spiritual gravity. We all want our businesses to be successful and provide us with so much: Income, security; a place to express our creativity, to work with others, to find meaning, to produce value for others, to find respect, and achievement. These are so important. Why would you not avail yourself and your business of the free resource that just happens to be the most valuable resource we could find? My friend, John, who founded and runs a very large and successful company, refers to God as his senior partner. He tells me that he has an office right next door to his. When he needs to he goes over, knocks on the door and lays out what he needs; what concerns him. It gives him much peace, power, knowledge, freedom, and success to let this stuff go into the hands of the guy who has all the talent, ability, and resources to solve his issue. When the economy was crumbling, John was in his usual positive mode. The outer situation didn't matter to him. He had the senior partner working for him. With his perspective, there was no reason to buy into a trend. He and his company did quite well. The first time he told me about his senior partner I listened with confusion. As he's talking I'm thinking. 'Didn't he start the business himself, with his wife?' 'I never heard him tell me about a partner, let alone a senior partner.' It took a few minutes for it to sink in and realize what he was talking about. Actually I'm going to stop writing for a few minutes. We are feeling tight financially these days, questioning our ability, why our business isn't doing better than it is. Are we missing something, is something wrong. So I'm going to go and lay down on the sofa in our office, right next to me, and do some talking to our senior partner. Heck I'll do it right here.

> *"Ok Louie, what the f- is going on. Why aren't we doing better financially? I would think by now we'd have a more consistent flow of business, more continual work, a deeper more consistent flow. I'd think we'd be more secure and confident in our pricing. I'd think I'd have more faith, more confident. I want to be giddy. Giddy in my faith. I read the words, robust faith yesterday and boy do I want to be that. I want to be a man of faith; of strong faith, to be optimistic, buoyant, happy, a good robust sense of humor, to laugh a lot, to be an it's going to work out fine kind of person. I want to feel good about our work and about our company—Proud of the success of our company financially, our impact on others, the clarity of what we do, what we are known for, our reputations, and the quality of our message. I want to be proud of it. I want to look at our check book and be proud, to be grateful, to feel alive, thriving, peaceful, and happy. When I think of myself and Tara as business people I want to be proud. I want to look in the mirror and feel good about myself, about our company, about the depth of my faith. I want to look in that mirror and laugh; a loud, robust laugh. When someone asks me about our company I want to say we are doing great and mean it; feel it. I want to feel secure, confident, and alive in our creativity knowing we are trying stuff and being confident in our success, in our process, in our progress.*

Sure it's going to work, why not.

3.24 Spiritual Practice

We often use the term *spiritual practice* to describe the ways in which we develop our spirituality and the spiritual tools that we use. Just like any other skill, we need to develop and cultivate this essential element—our spirit, and coming into alignment, attunement, realization, understanding of the divine and our spiritual nature; our purpose. The practice gives us a chance to hone the skills and develop the capacities to live a spiritual life: Through classic things like prayer and meditation, journaling, and yoga. But the list is so much more expansive and ready for us to develop new tools; new ways of practicing. This is why business is such a ripe breeding ground for us to practice. On one hand, business provides us with opportunities all day long to practice our full repertoire of spiritual tools. Spiritualty helps us clarify and move toward our goals. Our spiritualty can help us so much in navigating the myriad of relationships and interactions we have all day long. Our business lives provide us with so many challenges, frustrations, and unrealized expectations. Each one of these is another playground for us to test, practice, and develop our spiritual capacity. As a young teen my parents took me to Transcendental Meditation training. I was also introduced to the work of Jose Silva and the Silva method. This was an early start for me and to this day I continue to learn new concepts, practices, and exercises to develop and utilize my spiritual ability. It truly is an endless and very rich journey. Because work is so real time, it is such a perfect chance to unleash these tools. The demands for work are so high that it provides plenty of motivation to find better and better ways to work and to find peace, joy, and fulfilment in our work.

The work of Tich Nhat Hahn was the first that introduced me to the idea of using our everyday activities as a forum for our meditation. The idea of using the washing of dishes, or peeling an orange as a platform for meditation was a new concept for me. It was and is not hard to translate that into our daily work lives: a phone call, an email, a meeting, a project is each so ripe to play with. Each provides great opportunities to practice your spiritual ideas whatever they are. If being present in the moment is spiritual for you, then each of these moments are perfect opportunities. If you are into

God and prayer, then each of these are also wonderful chances for you to bring these powerful ideals to life. I have studied a lot about the use of intention setting and the power of thought. My cognitive behavioral training gets used all the time in work situations. Even my work with movement; yoga and tai chi, play themselves out beautifully in work situations. Meditations and prayer—I can't tell you how many times each day I use both. My work with spirituality and business is truly a broad canvas for me these days and I trust it will continue to drive my work endeavors for the rest of my life. We are currently planning our first spirituality in business executive retreat, which will take the course work I did with my MBA students and bring it more fully into the fabric of everyday work life. This is very exciting to me; the retreat and the opening up of this area of focus on my work. So many of us are already committed to spirituality in our lives and our work life is just waiting for us to unleash our spiritual gifts into her; let alone all of the folks who are turned off by religious and traditional spiritual practices. We are hoping that the non-religious element of work life will offer them a safe way to establish a spiritual life for themselves.

3.25 A Better Person

Our drive to continually become a better person—a better person at what we do and how we do it, for sure, but also a better person in who we are. Kinder, gentler, nicer—the things our mothers told us—the stuff of the Golden Rule.

Doesn't this apply in our work life too? Doesn't it seem obvious; a *no duh*. Why would we think that being a good person at work is somehow contrary to a strong bottom line and return on shareholder investment? Try this on. What if you believed that the best way to generate the best bottom line was to be the best person you could be; the most kind, generous, honest, loving person you could be. What if we could make this argument? What would you do then? Can you imagine how this would change the nature of business and business interactions?

3.26 Journey of the Spirit

What if the process of life is a journey of the spirit—a travel log. The whole thing is a journey of coming to understand our spirit, our purpose, and learn about our spirituality; reacting to its impulse, coming to do what it wants of us, coming to understand what we truly want and desire. A trip, and all that trips have to offer—new places to see, people to meet, learning new languages, cultures, dealing with frustration, overcoming difficult times, viewing amazing vistas. Wows, and mostly an experience of learning, of wonder, of joy. What if you believed this? Then where would work fit into your travel log of your spirit. It would have to fit somewhere, wouldn't it? Heck, we spend around 2000 hours a year doing it. It just seems so logical that we would include this part of our life in our spiritual life. It seems so obvious.

What if my amount of *enoughness* (E) is equivalent to my amount of peace of mind (P)?

$$E = P$$

Following this formula, if I want more peace, enjoyment, and happiness in my life, then I need to increase my *enoughness*. My *enoughness* is the lever, the causative agent, the root of my disease, and the root of my freedom. Isn't it good to know where to place our effort if we are looking for a result? If you want something, wouldn't it be very valuable to know exactly where to find it? You could think it is somewhere else and go looking there. You may even work very diligently and passionately in that place to get what you were looking for. You may even see all kinds of evidence of your labor. Like a big pile of dirt if you were digging a hole. But what a shame if you were digging in the wrong place, especially if you truly believe it was the right place. So imagine your joy, if somehow you came upon the knowledge that the place to dig was over there. It might take a bit to let go of all the effort you had placed in the hole you were digging, but if you truly came to believe that the place to dig was over there, wouldn't it be a relief to go dig in the place that contained what you truly wanted. Yes, you might feel some grief or resentment over lost time and energy. But maybe the source that told you where to now dig, also was able to tell you more. Like, now is the right time to dig there, or that your effort was not wasted, your past effort was training so that you'd be able to dig well in this new spot. It would give lots of loving and encouraging messages so that you would feel better about yourself. And so you go and you start to dig in this new place. For me, peace of mind has become more important to me than any other: Along with enjoyment and happiness. I am grateful to be digging in the place where they are. I am grateful to know that these are my primary goals. I am grateful. I wonder, about the connection between my sense of my *enoughness* and my peace of mind. It just seems logical to link them. This ratio of *enoughness* to *peace* seems so obvious. As well as the ratio between my *not enoughness* and the angst, anxiety, fear and *out of placeness* I have felt for so much of my adult life. It gives me relief and hope to watch my peacefulness increase, to see my spiritual life working— giving me more peace of mind; not just an idea but a reality.

3.27 A Coming out Party

Getting spirituality out of the closet and into the public. I've been afraid to let my clients know about my interest in spirituality. I've been afraid that it would weaken their perception of my ability to help them. I have a colleague, an accountant, who was afraid to let his clients know of his life as a musician because of the same fear. Here's the funny thing: I'd be more inclined to work with an accountant who had a passion for music. We hide our sweetest sides: Why, when there also lies so much of our power and brilliance. It's time to bring our spirituality out of the closet; to come front and center with it. So many of my students felt like they were the only ones who were hiding their spirituality, afraid to let it out in their jobs as bankers, engineers, and attorneys. I think the fear is something else too; a fear of being authentic, of being vulnerable, of letting people know who we truly are. By coming out, not only do we help ourselves, but we also make it easier for others to come out. We make it safer. The more we step forward, the more okay it becomes for others. It's not just for us. We have a responsibility to others, which only helps us because the more people who come out, the more it strengthens our own resolve and makes it ultimately easier for us to express it too.

3.28 Service

A life orientation that involves being of service to others. I see it as my real *job*, meaning that, regardless of my title—dad, sales guy, pizza maker—my real job, my real purpose, is to be of service to others and to God—the divine impulse and higher purpose. We get to play this out through our work. Work is a medium—a playground giving us a chance to play out a life of service; to develop the muscle for service, the discipline, in the face of *my* needs and other influences. Can I, can we, choose this service path? This leads to the practice…

3.29 Nourishment

This is a great word. It means to provide with food or other substances necessary for life and growth. It also means to maintain, to foster, to develop, to promote, and to keep alive. Yes, keep alive. This would be a pretty good thing for living organisms such as ourselves. If our lives are a journey of the spirit then we need some good nourishment along the way. Water and vegetables are pretty important for us, but on spiritual journeys, we also need spiritual nourishment. Divine water, divine food, and the substance of this divine life—information, inspiration, and hope.

3.30 Joy of Living

There are many ways to go through this life. Me, I'd prefer to have as much joy as possible. This has to be one of the promises of a spiritual life—more joy and finding the joy of living. I used to think that a spiritual life meant one of pain and suffering. This has more to do with my old image of God and what I thought God wanted from us. The more images I have of a loving and caring God who wants for me what I want and dream for myself, the more I can open myself to living joyously and being excited and enthusiastic about a spiritual life: One of fullness, abundance, a sense of meaning and purpose, of joy, fun, adventure, accomplishment, and the skills and tools to help me get through the inevitable tough times that life will bring.

3.31 Opening Doors

The more I broaden my definitions of spirituality, the broader the playing field becomes. One of my students talks about never meditating. Then, as we described the dynamics of meditation, he perked up. He had a *eureka* moment. "I've been meditating for years," he says. He is a competitive swimmer and he realized that the experience he often has when he is training is one of meditation: the breathing patterns, the repetitive strokes, and the sounds around him put him in a realized, tuned-in space. So how did he go from not meditating to meditating for years? We expanded his definition of meditation. We opened the door to more opportunities for meditation and ways of doing it. The same goes for prayer, God, the whole deal. As we open the doors, we give more people more ways to experience and cultivate their spiritual life.

3.32 Success

What does success look like? A full success, not just a number in our bank account, or a title at work, or success in sports. What if success is a peace of mind, a sense of harmony, loving family life, having friendships that matter, feeling a sense of purpose, and self-satisfaction?

3.33 We

Our spirituality does wonders for creating intimate, trusting bonds with other people. It gives us more compassion, empathy, and understanding. So many of us live lives of isolation. Not as hermits, but isolated emotionally and spiritually from others. Our clients, vendors, employees, team members, and family members can easily end up over there, in the *other* column. We don't feel connected.

As we develop spiritually, we open ourselves up and we connect in a more open way to others. The barrier between *us* and *them* starts to break down and we feel a greater sense of *we* in our world, and the world at large. The world started to feel safer to me. As I let you know who I am, how I feel; as I started to care for you, to look at our similarities, my world became safer because it had more *Wes*.

3.34 The Invisible Hand

Adam Smith got it right with the invisible hand stuff. What we need to add is that the invisible hand is a spirituality hand. So while this hand drives commerce, it has an even greater purpose: to drive life—the betterment of life. So when we add this element to our commerce, knowing that profit is a tool—just like fruit on a tree—for driving life, then we can unleash and throw ourselves into a work life that is fully-geared toward bringing spiritual principles to life.

3.35 God's Work at Work

Spirit at work. What if these values that many of us hold dear were the same values we passionately pursued in business? What if business became a vehicle for living and cultivating our highest values? Doesn't it seem ridiculous that we aren't already?

Here are a few of mine. This is the real meat of my life. It's seems absurd to not pursue them in my work. It seems absurd to not infuse my work with them too; not just for my own sake, but for the purpose of building a strong, resilient, meaningful business; for the sake of all the customers we can and do serve.

To live with faith and confidence

To have a clear sense of purpose and direction

To do the right things for the right reasons

To have hope

To care for others

To be kind and generous

To be helpful

To bring a spirit of love patience kindness forgiveness perseverance

To be honest and open-minded

To be resilient

To be smart

To be relevant

To be patient and enduring.

Why shouldn't words like fellowship, common good, and love become part of our common business lexicon.

3.36 God's Work

Doing God's will—why do I assume that that has to be painful and arduous? I have been taught that doing God's will requires really hard work, some suffering, probably some poverty, lacking; stuff like that. I'm not sure how these images got into my head, but that is my first reaction. If it isn't painful, it won't count as Godly work. Intellectually, I know this is not true, but as I dig under the surface, this is the story I tell myself. I have to conjure up the image that this could be a joyous experience, an energizing experience, even possibly an easy experience. No wonder I'm resistant to doing God's will. Who wants to volunteer for pain, hardship, and suffering? I want to open my mind to the possibility that I can do God's will and gain that positive karmic kick from doing God's work and do it in the spirit of ease, and joy. It would be so much easier to align with God if we could imagine this as an uplifting and energizing experience rather than one that is simply painful.

3.37 Unholy

What if the flooded basement, the serious illness, or the hardship of depression were all holy? I'm afraid to accept this possibility. I don't want to see the pain in life as part of the whole; the holy whole. I'd rather keep images of feeling peaceful, of feeling in the right place; focused, present, engaged, healthy, joyful. I want this to be the image of rightness; of holiness. No pain. To do so, rejects so much of our lives. Our lives are guaranteed to be painful at times. If these parts are not holy, then we are rejecting so much of ourselves. We are rejecting life. We are rejecting God.

3.38 But Why?

Why do I resist accepting all of this, especially the discomfort? The disease as part of the whole; as part of the holy. Why hold onto a dream that just causes me more discomfort? Not only the discomfort of the situation, but also the added tension of judging it as not right; which means that I must not be right enough, or life is not right enough, or God is not right enough. Why am I doing this? I live with this fantasy as a way to protect myself. As long as I keep up this fantasy, then I can protect myself from living with the reality that troubling times will come upon me or my family. Rather than facing a reality that includes pain and developing the resources to handle it, I try to escape into a fantasy. Again I'm afraid that I am not enough to handle it. So I better find some way of avoiding it. I'm trying to find some way to control what I know I can't. Struggle is my payment. Look how hard I'm trying. It is proof that I am doing my part. What I really want is control. What I really want is protection. But if I don't believe that God is enough, then I need to look elsewhere. I need to find some way to get my needs met.

3.39 More Unholy

What we call imperfect is actually perfect and whole. If you believe God is enough, then God can only create *enough*. There cannot be imperfection. So the disease I feel is not a sign of me not being enough—or you, or life, or God, not being enough. The disease must be part of the *enough*, the perfection, the rightness—it must be holy. Maybe our *not enoughness* is holy, too?

3.40 Nothing to Prove

Let's play a little game today. What if I have nothing to prove today? That's right, nothing to prove. I'm going to a meeting with a bunch of high-level execs. They have invited me to meet with them. I think it's about their university. Maybe they want my advice or maybe they want me to help them. Now what if I go in there with a feeling of nothing to prove? What might that look like? I'm not talking arrogance; I'm talking about confidence. I know that I am there for a reason. I know that what I have to bring to the table is enough, good, helpful, and real. What if I don't need this work? What if I have enough and even without this work I have enough? What if we all have enough and will continue to have enough? What would happen then? How would this impact my demeanor, what I say, and how I say it? I've got to believe that it will free me up to be more honest, to share more forthrightly, to be less afraid of saying something that would make me lose this, that would piss them off, or offend them. When I feel that I need it, then I will probably play it safe and not say anything too strong that would make them uncomfortable or challenge them. But if I'm enough, and I have enough, and all is good enough, then maybe I am more willing to speak a truth as I see it, to say what I truly believe, or base my opinion on what I'm hearing and on my experience. If I'm enough, then I'll be able to listen better, too. I don't have to listen simply looking for an opportunity to benefit myself. I can listen more intently to them—to their cares and their needs. And If I believe that they have nothing to prove, that they are good enough, then I can listen even more clearly. I can learn from them. I can allow my instincts to take over. In this state, we can create something that is enough; that is beautiful and real and powerful and perfect for this situation.

Today I don't have to fantasize about how much I can get out of this situation. I can dream about what we can create; what good we can create. I can be open to opportunities to care, to help, and to provide for my family. I've got to believe that if I have nothing to prove, then I open myself up to get the greatest opportunity. I've got to believe that I can be of maximum help. I've got to believe that I will feel more confident, more crisp, more decisive, and more alive. I've got to believe that I'm more valuable to them in this way. I've got to believe that we are more valuable to each other this way. If I've got nothing to prove, then I've probably got nothing to lose.

This could be a fun game. I'm tired of feeling like I need to prove something, to prove myself, how much I need this, or feeling like a fake in some way. I want to feel that I deserve to be at the table; that I'm at this table for a reason; for a higher reason. That a higher power has brought us together at this time. Why now? Because each of us has been and are on our own journeys. So we are meeting exactly at this time for a reason; for a choreographed reason. If neither of us has anything to prove, then we can sit there as equals; as fellows. We can be intentional in our help for each other. Imagine that. What if we truly sat as equals with nothing to prove? We can be there to help one another and help each other have the greatest possible impact on this situation and on life as a whole. Imagine that. Fellows working together; playing together. Imagine what we can create and imagine the quality of what we'd create. Not just the thing, but the quality of our interaction. An interaction produced by *enoughness* and trust from creation. Now that is cool: The *what-if* of our interaction, the fun, the ease, the sense of purpose. Now that is cool. Imagine all of the extras and promotions that will emerge from this as we unleash each other's talents and unleash them upon each other. We will be more open with our needs, our concerns, our solutions, our resources, and our contacts. This is getting pretty good. It's not by some chance that we are meeting. Obviously, by the design of life we are ready to meet now; today. And let's believe that design is good enough. Good enough for a good purpose; or even a grand purpose. What if we are meeting to participate in a grand, wonderful, life-affirming, trust-filled purpose? A good, wholesome, grand, and wonderful purpose? What if that is why we are getting together? What a blessing. What a cool thing to do. What is that reason—not only for each of us, but also for the organizations we represent, for all the people we represent, and all the situations that we will face? There is some reason and I believe it is for some good. What might I help today? What might I hear that helps me? God, please help me be enough today, or better yet, realize that I'm enough today, that we have enough, and these guys are enough, and that You are enough and this life You have created for us is enough. Let today be enough. I'm curious to hear and to see what will happen. Please let me listen with love, with compassion, with power, and with clarity. Let me be open to all the opportunities that will be here for me, for our family, for our business, and for our future. Please let us create something real and big and wonderful to know that we are participating in the betterment of life and of people's lives in society. Please let us know that we are playing a part in fulfilling the *enoughness* of life; of this life. Let's just see what can happen if we all have nothing to prove today. Let's see how much fun we can have together.

3.41 Lubrication

WD-40 is amazing. You can use it for so many stuck situations: bicycle chains, door locks, sliding doors. Did you know that it can even be used on clothing stains? When I think of despair, I think of being stuck. When I have felt despair, it sure seemed like there was no way out. What has helped me the most is getting vulnerable, taking the risk to ask for help, telling someone the truth about my situation, and sharing how I feel. This truth-telling may have even more uses than WD-40. Truth and vulnerability are amazing lubricants. Without them, it is impossible to play for real.

3.42 Higher Power

Imagine having fun and playing with our higher power. So that, when I'm having fun, playing, being engaged—that is when I am doing the right thing, doing God's will, serving my purpose. Once I was with a client, a CEO, taking a walk. We talked about his role; what it is, his purpose, his passion; that kind of stuff. Where is he most useful to his company, to himself, and to his family? Well, what if it were easy to tell? What if we looked at what parts of his work give him the most joy, when he is most engaged, and what is most fun for him? What if that stuff was his most important stuff to do? Could we allow our joy indicator to also be our indicator of our best, our most valued, our highest power kind of endeavors? Could this be possible? I'm going to NYC this morning to meet a client. I'm feeling a little tightness in my chest. I prayed to God; help me have fun. Could that be why I'm going? Part of me rejects this. It can't be enough. But could having fun be the best thing I could do to promote our company, to serve [George], to build our wealth, to grow, and to do work we are really good at? Can I trust the fun? Imagine that my higher power isn't some guy in a beard. Could my higher power be fun? I can't even imagine what prayer looks like when that is my higher power. I guess a laugh, a chuckle, helping others have fun, and having as much fun as possible regardless of the situation or how I'm feeling. So even if I'm not feeling playful, I can desire it, I can add a little play; to my face, to my words. I could try something new, take another route, do something differently, get vulnerable, tell someone how I am feeling.

4

A Non-Struggle Theology

4.1 Getting the Good Stuff

Our addiction to struggle comes from the stories we were told about being good, about getting rewarded, and ultimately getting salvation; as in getting to heaven. I'm not sure what came first, the stories about what God wants from us or our belief about what our Gods, our parents, and our bosses and authorities of all forms want from us. Who put these concepts into the iconic stories we were told about life; our purpose? How do we get the really good stuff in life while we are here and the good stuff comes after this life? Many of us want to know what formulas we need to follow in order to get the lives we want, the wealth we want, the relationships, the health and the happiness we desire—you know; the good stuff in life. It's not a new game. Our attempts at achieving all this good stuff include some wonderful, books like: *The Seven Habits of Highly Successful People, The Road Less Traveled, The Secret,* and *The 10 Commandments.* Aren't all of these and many more sources trying to teach us how to get and keep that good stuff? Over history, we have had teachers, gurus, and preachers each helping us distill the formulas that we need to follow in order to lead successful lives.

For me, the big problems are the stories they told us that reinforce and promulgate the idea of struggle, and desire for pain and hardship. These struggle stories are the foundation of our current *no-pain no-gain* philosophy. I am concerned with the stories that teach us the idea that pain itself is a virtue to cultivate. I am not anti-pain. Pain has had a tremendous positive value in my life. The drive to find relief from pain is the fuel for change that many of us need at times in our life. The experience of pain is one of the greatest motivators to find peace of mind, joy, and happiness.

But this is not a reason to embrace pain and struggle as a way of life.

I have come to realize that God wants me to be joyous. These days I'm very attracted to the idea that our purpose in life is joy. That God created us to be joyous; that our nature is peace. That our goal is to enjoy life; not endure life.

I was not raised in a Bible-thumping family. I went to synagogue every Sabbath morning and evening. I went to after-school programs at the synagogue three days a week and we followed the holidays. I don't think of my early life as a religious one. The influence of my religious teaching and our Jewish culture deeply impacted my internal guidance system. This guidance system runs so deeply and naturally that I rarely realize it is running. In the same way that while my heart has beaten my whole life, I am not too aware of the deep internal systems that run my heart and its beating. This is why reflection is such an important part of a spiritual life. It gives us the opportunities to see what is driving us and if those values are in alignment with whom we care to be. It is a bit shocking and surprising for me to see that the Biblical, religious, and cultural stories of my heritage have such a deep impact on how I live.

While these days I am drawn to a life of joy, many of the stories I was raised on taught a very different idea. They taught and built the very foundation of my addiction to struggle and my deification of pain. These stories may even be idolatrous in the sense that pain itself is so honored and worshipped. This is the foundation of the struggle conspiracy. Moses hits the rock and can't go into Israel as his punishment, our whole myth of slavery in Egypt, Joseph thrown into the hole, Abraham being asked to sacrifice his son; and there are so many more. Then there are our holidays; so many of which are related to suffering, to our people being harmed and enslaved; our Temples and cities destroyed—over and over again historically. As a child at summer camp and throughout our culture we observed the holocaust deeply. I had no idea how impactful these stories, studies, and worships were building a deep commitment to struggle—each one like a building block, building the internal shrines for the need, the honor of pain; pain as our protector, pain as our heritage, pain as the inevitable path of our lives, and pain as God's *gift*.

And it's not just the stories of our past. The struggle myth is alive and well in our time as well.

Notice the stories we use these days to honor folks. Notice how many of them are related to *how hard they worked, all they had to overcome, the sacrifices they made.* So many of our current success myths are wrapped around the struggle. Think of the stories you honor in others. How many of them carry the theme, *it's much better to succeed without talent but on hard work.* Think of the stories you tell about yourself; especially when you are trying to explain or validate yourself.

I worked so hard today.

I had to overcome so much.

My back is killing me.

I was sick but I showed up anyway.

My plate is so full.

I wish I could stay but I have to get to my meeting.

They ask so much of me.

You really have to look at this for yourself. You will be shocked at how much you use struggle to justify and prove your own worth— or use your struggle as an excuse for not doing something. It is a great procrastination tool. It makes you look busy, but in reality you are avoiding what you really need to be doing, or what you are afraid to do. Be careful in reading this stuff, because you truly may not want to give up your struggle and the *gifts* it gives you.

The more I started to see the impact of my life myth stories, I had an idea. Could I rewrite these stories to tell a non-struggle story? What if I took the struggle out of the stories, what might the stories look like? Since these stories are so powerful in creating struggle, they must have the same power to build more ease, joy, and happiness. I bet I could help remove the struggle in my life if I removed the struggle from the stories I tell myself; the stories we honor. And, I can increase my joy by increasing the joy inherent in our mythic stories. Imagine if we told success stories of ease. Imagine if we told stories of success achieved in peace. How about having accomplishment in joy? If we believe that *Ease = Genius*, then let's tell stories that provide evidence of genius in ease.

Unfortunately, ease, joy, and peace are actually looked down upon as a lesser form of being than hardship.

On one hand we desire these qualities and at the same time we diminished their value. If we look at what we truly value, then hardship will trump joy every time. It's obvious. Watch the stories that support what we honor and cherish most. You've got to check this out for yourself. Notice the stories you tell to prove your worth. Notice the stories we tell as a society when we are trying to demonstrate achievement and honor. For me it has been a shocking revelation to see how we honor struggle.

I really hope these stories inspire your to rewrite your own life stories. I want to read, hear, and listen to stories that promote our enoughness, that teach us, for me, that life is safe, secure, and peace filled. I want stories that reinforce that we live in abundance and prosperity; stories that teach that we are blessed; that we are born into this life form for goodness, joy, and liberation.

Our stories create our reality. We can change our stories to create the life we want to live. We can create stories to serve our deepest dreams for our lives.

If you are like me, you may feel like you are doing something wrong. In changing the story, you may even feel like you are going to get punished or go to hell. Trust me, I have those feelings and thoughts too. I'm grateful. I now have the freedom to play with my stories. I have the courage to rewrite them. Here are four stories taken from the Hebrew and New Testaments. I hope they get you going by opening up your mind and heart to telling stories that free you up. Enjoy. Let me know what you think. I hope they feel good to you. I hope they make you smile. I really hope you are inspired to write your own.

4.2 Original Choice

What if we got the Adam and Eve story wrong? I wanted to see if I could take away the idea of being human equals being bad and in disharmony with each other, with us, and with nature. I wanted to remove any idea of *original sin*. I want to create a story of harmony; that we are in harmony with one another and with the process of life. I also wanted to reinforce the idea of choice. That we get to choose the game of life and the way we live our lives. I wanted a greater sense of freedom and ease in the story; not to take ourselves too seriously. I'd like to use our myth story to bring a greater sense of levity to my life—more ease, friendship, and joy. Let's change this iconic story's theme to *original choice*. Enjoy!

Setting: The Garden of Eden. There is a tree, an apple, a serpent, and two naked people. The three of them were hanging out like they do every day; they were buddies. They had just finished playing a game and were chilling out under one of their favorite trees. Then the snake dude had a very intriguing idea.

> **Snake Dude:** *Hey you guys, do you want to try out this being human thing?*
>
> **Eve:** *What does it entail?*
>
> **Snake Dude:** *You get to try all kinds of cool stuff, learn life experiences, meet all kinds of people, make mistakes, and spend your time on an adventure getting back to here.*
>
> **Adam:** *Is it an all-or-nothing option?*
>
> **Snake Dude:** *No way, you always get to choose it again and again. You can stop whenever you want or play as many times as you want. And, you get to come back here too.*
>
> **Adam:** *What do you think, Eve?*
>
> **Eve:** *Do we still get to have the sex thing?*
>
> **Snake Dude:** *Sure*
>
> **Adam and Eve:** *Ok. Let's do it.*
>
> **Eve:** *What's next?*
>
> **Snake Dude:** *Just bite into this apple and the game is on.*
>
> **Adam:** *Cool...*

4.3 In the Beginning

The Biblical creation story seems so impersonal to me. God is creating all this stuff alone. Humans don't even get into the story until the very end of the week. I'd like to create a version of the creation story where the creative process is a joyous thing, a communal expression; a bunch of really creative forces and resources coming together to make something special. My hope is that this will lead to a more joyous life for us creations. Tara and I use a simple and profound concept in our work. *People support a world they help to create.* I think God would have more fun with some buddies, with his creations, if they got to participate in the process of creation. I also want to use this story to break through the concept of work as drudgery. I want stories to help me see work as a joyous creative process. I want stories to reinforce our ability to work together well and enjoyably; to see work as fun, rewarding, and meaningful. I'd like to reinforce that we are naturally very good at what we do and that we create wonderful things that are enduring. Great sex has to be one of the ultimate pleasures in life—especially with someone you love and trust—the real intimate, fun, passionate kind of thing. Just think how great God sex must be. Wow. So let's try another version of In the Beginning.

In the beginning they just touched. A real gentle sensual touch; in one of those spots that just makes you tingle all over. The Gods had sex and it was awesome. The scientists are right; there was a big bang. A real big bang and it shot forth a divine seed into a divine egg. The explosive force was great and set in motion a thrashing of chemicals, electricity, stuff of all kinds; whirling, flying, bombarding, crashing into forms of all kinds. To the eye it would have looked incredibly chaotic and wild, but inside was a design, a formula and planned integrating of myriads of stuff and forces, each driving towards forms, live forms of all kinds each bumping into one another and creating more form, more forms; our life crashing into being. We can try to describe it in a 7-step sequence, but it is so much bigger, grander; more subtle than our logical minds can comprehend. But our hearts; our souls understand completely. We were there. We were in the story. Our creation and creative process is still unraveling right before our eyes. Divine fornication leading to divine form, leading continually to more formation; creation is still emerging from that grand evening, all from the most subtle, sweet, beautiful, sensual touch.

And on the 7th day we rested together. It felt like a 6-day love affair. When we were done we rested that sweet beautiful cuddly rest that comes after the most sweet, erotic, passionate love making. As we laid together we looked back on what we had done; on what we created, what we experienced, and with a sigh of joy we said, "That was good. Really good."

Creation of all kinds seems to work this way. Seeds hit the fertile ground—the oak tree does it that way, the aperiodic worm does it, even rain in the clouds—an interaction of two becoming one becoming many. Creation has power, unleashed energy, and transformation. Ideas emerge this way, as do organizations. The power, the feelings, the passion, the intimacy, the fun, the *allness*; and the other worldliness of it. Imagine all of that on a divine level, to the max—full, divine fornication. Wow…not only the act itself, but the creation, the perfect creation of the divine. It can only be divine; two divine creatures creating one. How do you pray to this fornicating God? What does that look like?

4.4 'Moses; Hit It!'

This story has always been disturbing to me. Moses was amazing. He dedicated himself to his people and the call from God. Then, because he hits the rock instead of talking to it, he gets a big punishment. So I wanted to rewrite this story. I wanted more joy in the story; more reward. I also want a story that reinforces the fact that we are human, we make mistakes, our faith fails at times, we lose our patience and that it's ok. It's ok to be human. In being human we are loved. We are loved by God and it's still ok to love ourselves. It's ok to laugh at our mistakes and stay buoyant. Mostly I wanted to represent a picture of God that is appealing for me. I wanted to a God who is loving, forgiving, understanding, and playful. I want a buddy God not a punishing God. Enjoy.

And God said to Moses, "Hit it, dude, hit it. Smack the hell out of it."

And the Israelites cheered, "Go, Moses, Go Moses, Go, Go."

The band continued playing, the place erupted as Moses held his guitar high, held it over his head, smiled at the audience and—

boom—he brought it down, smashing against the boulder. KA-Boom. The sound was loud and strong, reverberating throughout the crowd, echoing off the mountains. You could feel the rush, everyone did and them—boom—the geyser came erupting out of the rock. Fresh, vibrant, cool water came flowing out of a rock. The dry ground was drenched with flowing water. The people jumped into it, drank it, filled jugs with it, created pools and cisterns, drains, baths, sprinklers, and irrigation. The whole place came alive, full of green growing stuff, schools of fish, butterflies, trees, and bees. All kinds of wildlife, birds, and herds came to it. The place erupted into life. The rock smiled as it released its life force. The other rocks saw what was going on and joined in. It felt great to release all that pent up hydrogen and oxygen. It felt really good. Giddy good. Refreshing good. Hopeful. Transcendent. Refreshing, cool, hip, alive. It felt really good. They were thankful to Moses. Wow, now this was living.

The Israelite brethren saw what was possible and they too took their hands, their staffs, and their feet, and started drumming on rocks, dancing on rocks, chucking rocks, and more and more water came forth. The dry, desolate, barren area became chock full of life and everyone rejoiced. The rocks, the people, and the water had a ball.

God was happy and said unto Moses, "You've done good, brother, thanks for the help." And Moses said, "Hey, God-dude, I'm getting kind of old and this place feels really great. My kids are here, my grandkids, I can make a good life here. I think I'd rather stay here. Let the young ones head over there and start their own thing. What do you think of that? This way they have a home base to come home to."

And God said to Moses, "I hadn't thought of that idea. It's great. Let's go with that." And then God called out to Joshua, "Hey, Josh, do you got a minute? We have an idea for you. I think you guys will really love this one."

4.5 The Ongoing Supper

Jesus invited a bunch of his buddies over for dinner. It was an amazing night: Great food, great friends, and wonderful conversation. It was an important night, one they celebrated every month. For the past 10 years they had been gathering like this, to love each other, to celebrate the joy of being alive; to share their fears, their hopes, and their dreams. They came together for each other, for themselves; but mostly for their desire to be positive influences in the lives of others. They came to talk about God and worship, being of service, how to make the world a better place; and how to help others find their potential, their love, and their connection to their God.

They had this wonderful ritual of washing each other's feet. It was an act of love, of reverence, and intimacy for one another. It was symbolic of the role they played in life—caring for one another, going out into the world, caring for those around them, and helping them live clean, uplifting, and joyous lives. Tonight was one of many—many that had come before and many that were still to come.

They called these gatherings, *The Last Supper*. They did so for their sense of urgency. What if this was our last one? They wanted to live and serve with passion, gusto, and meaning. If this *was* their last supper, then they could be assured that they'd truly shared their love, their hope, their hearts, and their fears without reservation. Being together at a Last Supper insured that this supper and every one they had afterward would be awesome. So they came together with hope and gratitude for this: their Last Supper.

4.6 Jesus Gets Anxious Too

> **Jesus:** *I'm feeling really nervous.*
>
> **Bob:** *What are you worried about most?*

Jesus: I'm afraid I'll be standing there up at Olive Mount all by myself. Will anyone show up today? Will they like what I say? Will I look like a fool? Is it the same stuff they've already heard? Will it have any impact? Stuff like that.

Bob: Well, what is the worst that can happen? Does it really matter if anyone shows up? It's not like your career depends on it.

Jesus: Yeah, that's a good way to look at it.

Bob: My friend, Donald, told me that when he talks to a group he focuses on one person; just one person who might get some help from his message. That way, he doesn't have to worry about impressing people or what they will think of him. It's guaranteed that someone will show up, even if it's just one person. If you tell the truth and speak from your heart, they are bound to hear something that will help them today.

Jesus: Umm, thanks, Bob. I'm glad I'm not the only one who feels this way.

Bob: What time are things getting started at the Mount, I'll try to come. Hey, it might be real memorable.

4.7 The Stories We Tell Ourselves

My friend Donald told me to be real careful about what I tell myself. As much as we are instructed by our mythic life stories we are directed by the stories we tell ourselves. Currently Tara and I are struggling with our business in terms of earning enough money. It feels like a scary time, we are not sure what to do. And If I get quiet, I will hear the stories we are telling ourselves; 'We are in trouble.' 'We don't know what to do, this is too hard, it won't work, we should have done something sooner.' These voices are not always readily heard. They run quietly most of the time; behind the scenes. Often when I do hear them, they seem so true that I don't realize they are a story; a version that I am telling myself. Little do I realize that I am telling myself this. I have told myself these kinds of stories for so much of my life that there is no gap between the story and the idea that they are just thoughts. They may not be true. Just like the stories of our youth. We can change and play with the stories that we tell ourselves. This is what Donald meant. "Evan, be careful, pay attention to what you are telling yourself." I often forget or am unaware that I have a choice. That I can choose what I am going to tell myself. I can reflect and decide if what I am telling myself is helpful or harmful. What about our current situation. What might change if I/we changed the stories we were telling ourselves. What if I told myself that we are doing fine, that we will, and do, know what we are doing; that we are taking appropriate action, that we are smart, that we are hardworking, that fate is on our side, that we are on the brink of our great success, that God is helping us right now, that we are in good hands. What would change if we changed our stories? What impact does our self story telling have on our attitude, our life orientation, our experience of life, our choices, and our results based on the stories we tell ourselves. I think you can see what I see. The stories of fear; the, *I'm telling myself about not doing enough, of falling apart,* are stories based in *not good enough.* Aren't they the residue of our fear; or is fear the residue of *not good enough.* Do the fear voices, the easier stories derive from the source of *not good enough.* What stories might I tell myself from a source of *good enough?* From a source of being loved by the source of creation from the source of loving myself. What stories will I tell myself from a source of love?

> *Evan, I love you.*
>
> *Evan, I am taking care of you.*
>
> *Evan, you have gotten through tough times before and you will this time.*
>
> *Evan, tell someone what you are going through.*
>
> *Evan, ask for help.*
>
> *Evan, do what you can today.*

Evan, trust me.

Evan, trust yourself.

Evan, trust yourself.

What will change in how we handle and respond to our current situation if we tell our *self-loving*, hopeful, encouraging, positive stories. What will change in our attitude, our decisions, our results; if we can change the stories. The fear I feel is that the stories of fear will move me into positive action. This fear voice tells me that stories of hope will drive me to take soft, or no, action. I can't trust them to get us out of a jam. This is part of how they feed our addiction to struggle. I believe that I need them. I need the struggle to get me safe, to get me out of danger. But this too is just a story. Another story that I can change. If I see it as a story; I can choose to change it. I can have some freedom. I can counter the fear story again with a faith story.

Evan, faith will work. Faith will work, Faith takes courage. Look at your own life, look at the lives of so many stories I have heard; The stories of hope I have heard in my life.

I can recall the stories, the real stories of hope, of redemption of people changing from one condition of lack to a condition of prosperity. I can listen, I can repeat, I can ask for these stories. I can bolster myself with stories of hope: Real stories of hope. I can ask some friends to remind me of my stories. I can ask them their stories. "How did you get through that?" I can choose to strengthen my faith, to strengthen my muscle of faith, of hope, of courage. I can look at this situation and choose a story of strength. This situation will improve. This is a chance for me to learn, to learn about what is mine and what is Gods. I can learn how to let go. I can learn about how to take action in faith. This moment in time is a great gift. We all move through it as we have in the past, We all get to the other side. We will be better, stronger, more grounded, more healed. There is healing to go on here, if not this wouldn't be happening. This is a great time. A great time. A great time to heal, to grow, to prosper. This is the story I am starting to tell myself.

As Donald told me, we have to be cognizant of the stories we tell ourselves because they have such an impact on the quality and success of our lives. If I want more joy, more peace, and more love, then I need to tell myself more stories of joy, peace, and love. It is why affirmations are so important. They are a way we can create the lives we want. They help us heal from the negative stories we tell ourselves and they help us cultivate and grow the life we want to live. These affirmations are our way of choosing the stories we want to tell ourselves. Donald, thank you!

> *I love to write.*
>
> *I love to create.*
>
> *I am a wonderful writer.*
>
> *I trust my writing.*
>
> *I trust the words that come through me.*
>
> *I trust myself.*
>
> *I trust myself.*

4.8 Which Version?

When I was about 5 or 6 years old, my mom got me a pair of shorts that I loved. We were out shopping together and I saw these shorts. I loved them. She bought them for me. I was excited when I got home and ran upstairs to cut off the label. I couldn't wait to put them on. In my excitement, or in being 5, I cut a hole in my pants when I was cutting off the label. I felt terrible.

As I recall my mom was mad at me. The story I took from this was that it's dangerous to be excited or enthusiastic. I told myself, "If I get excited I'll make a mistake and screw something up." This belief did not stem from this one story, there were many situations where I got excited, enthusiastic, pumped up and then got in some form of trouble. It happened in school quite often from grades 1 through 7. I talked a lot in class. I'd get in trouble for it. Maybe I was bored, or anxious, or simply very talkative. I didn't experience myself as a bad or a naughty kid. I don't recall talking to get attention. My talking emanated from a place inside me—to me, a good place; a joyous place. I don't recall the kids minding, but most of my teachers did. Their punishing reaction to me, made me feel out of control, bad, hollow; a person lacking depth, discipline, or substance. I felt like a fool inside; insecure. I told myself, 'If only I could keep quiet, settle down, be more grown up, more mature.' I was telling myself many versions of 'I'm not good enough.' In 7th grade, the prettiest girl I had even seen like me as I liked her. I was great at sending her notes, but got all tied up, embarrassed if I tried to talk to her one-on-one. In reflection, I was telling myself some version of, 'I can't believe why she would like me' which is another version of 'I'm not good enough.'

This same *not good enough* version is manifested in all areas of my life. When I applied to Rabbinical School this voice rang clear; when I was interested in a woman, when I wanted to start a business. I had an equation of enthusiasm = danger, but I couldn't see it.

I shut down all areas of my enthusiasm. I didn't understand the connection to my *not good enough* stories. I didn't even realize it was enthusiasm I was reacting to. I just saw a connection between me trying stuff and the pain that came with it. San Francisco, Rabbinical School, relationships, innovative ideas; all seemed to get me in trouble. I remember telling myself, 'stop trying anything new, anything exciting. Shut it off Evan, shut it off.' What I was really trying to shut off was me. I didn't realize that is wasn't my light that was getting me in trouble, it was the *not good enough* version of my life. My enthusiasm would bubble up and my inner protector, would shout; 'Stop, stop, this will get us in trouble again.' But I misinterpreted this voice. What I heard is, 'Evan, this is a bad idea, stop, stop. This is dangerous.'

Unfortunately, most of my inner voice was coming from my interpretation of how *authorities* reacted to me: Parent, teacher, girl I liked, boss. I took their reaction as a rejection of me. I interpreted their reaction to mean *I'm not good enough*. Their reactions to me took on a lot of power because the *me* that was being rejected was my core *me*; my enthusiastic *me*. I took their reactions to heart. 'I', my deep 'I' must be really off; not trustworthy. I could not see that my 'I' was triggering their fear; that much of their reactions to me were based on their fear, their *not good enough*. I got it wrong. I took their *not good enough* to mean I'm *not good enough*. And thus, I started telling myself, many versions of *I'm not good enough*.

My friendteacher, Donald, told me, "Evan, be careful what you tell yourself." I did not appreciate the power of his words at first. If I tell myself that I'm not good enough, then it will manifest in ways that will sabotage my ability to achieve. This inner voice is so powerful that it will trump our surface attempts to do that thing—Even in the face of great effort. The inner voice, what we tell ourselves, will win out until we are able to change that voice. So much of this book is about identifying that voice and its impact and then learning how to switch it from *not good enough* to *love*; from struggle to freedom.

> *I trust myself.*
>
> *I am smart.*
>
> *I am talented.*
>
> *I am a good friend.*

4.9 The Re-Write

We can go back and rewrite our stories; relive them in a way that will fuel our confidence, our *good enough* and our delight in ourselves. Bob once told me that we have to teach our brains to be our best friends. If *what we tell ourselves* is so powerful, why not use this power for our good. Here is a rewrite of the *hole-*

in-my-pants story. It gives me such good energy to do the rewrite and then gives me more good energy and insight to re-read it. We can create our own mythology. Why not write and tell stories that bolster our enthusiasm, our joy, our peace, and our good thoughts about our most *preciousdelightful* selves.

4.10 Pants I Love

> *Scene: Evan, 5 years old, is crying; holding a pair of shorts in one hand and a pair of scissors in the other.*
>
> ***Evan:*** *Mah mee, Mah mee, I cut my pants, I cut my pants (he trusts his mommy enough to let her know, he is sure, from past experience that she will consul him, be kind to him and love him very much).*
>
> ***Mom:*** *Here, Here. Let me see my little one.*
>
> ***Evan:*** *I I I I lllllllove these pants so, so, so, so much Mahhhh Meee (the words barely come out over his crying).*
>
> ***Mom:*** *It's ok Evee; it's ok. It's just a little hole, I make mistakes too. We can fix them or even better, I know what to do (she pulls him close to her, puts him on her lap, gives him a hug and kisses him on the top of his head).*
>
> ***Mom:*** *Let's go back and get another pair. I'm sure they have one. This time I'll let the lady cut the tag off and you can put the pants on right in the store. What do you think of that?*
>
> ***Mom:*** *I love you so much Evan!*
>
> *My mommy loves me very much.*
>
>
> *It's ok to make mistakes.*
> *I feel so much better now.*
> *Wow, don't I look handsome?*

5

Brilliance, Love, and Grace

5.1 Why do I have negative thoughts?

I sit down to write. I had an idea that I'm excited to write about. But my mind tells me that I can't write it, it's too hard to describe, I'm not capable of writing it well. The usual chatter.

The other day I prayed on this type of thinking. In particular, I was having fearful thoughts about my children and was worried about them getting seriously ill. In those moments, in that mode of thinking, it almost seems normal, average, to assume that they will get some serious illness. I took it to prayer. I went inside myself and asked, why would I think this way? They are my thoughts. Why would I think like this? As I have gotten to know myself—through much reading, reflection, prayer; many, many conversations, and many hours of listening to others' stories, I have come to believe that everything about us is divine. I'm almost afraid to write these words.

If this is true, even my negative thoughts have a purpose. This is what I am coming to understand. My thoughts are part of me; part of me as a living organism. As a living organism, endowed with life by the divine, I am totally geared toward life. Why would God create us in any other way? The tree, the brook, the flower, the moth, us; we are all alive, filled with this life force. There is no opposing force, nothing about us that is geared toward destruction. Our destructive tendencies emerge from misconception, misbeliefs about our purpose, about scarcity, and about our need to protect ourselves. Somehow we have forgotten that we are children of the divine; that we are truly alive, fully alive, provided for, given everything we need, full of life, full of wisdom. Somehow we have forgotten that our purpose is to live, to be fulfilled, to live in radiant health, to thrive. That is our nature. But instead, we focus on the disease, we focus on the pain, we focus on the lack, and we think that is the way it is supposed to be. So we scramble, we make things hard, we defend, we protect, we attack ourselves and others out of our misconceptions. But I have come to believe that this is not the way it really is. We have allowed ourselves to become the way we are by virtue of the way we think and what we have come to believe. We think it needs to be hard. So we make it hard.

I was having one of these moments, when my mind was caught in fearful thinking—in this case, about my children. I went into meditation. What is my purpose? Why am I choosing to think this way? Lately my first step is brilliance. I have come to realize that the force behind this action—even this fear-filled, worrisome thinking—is brilliance. It has to be. The brilliance of the creator, manifested in me, in my thinking capacity. Its essence is brilliance. This feels much more empowering to me than to think of my thinking as sick, withered, wrong, or some form of anti-life. That is how I used to think of my negative moments or attributes. Somehow they were a foreign entity, separate from me, separate from my life force. They needed to be changed, eradicated, removed. But now I see them as brilliance, as stemming from brilliance, not foreign. I don't have to resist them, or remove them, or run from them. Brilliance.

The next piece that I know for sure is that it is misdirected brilliance. From my belief system, developed over years of influence—upbringing, parents, teachers, society—I have taken on certain beliefs. These beliefs, like a sculptor to clay, fashion the brilliance; our brilliance. So my beliefs have shaped my thinking and turned brilliance into thoughts of fear and worry. In this case; about my children. This brilliance, our brilliance, has one purpose: life, to promote, sustain, to enliven. That is our purpose. That is what we are geared to do; to live. Even at our worst, when we may think we are in self-sabotage mode, what we are really doing is moving full force toward life; toward sustaining life. We have the same power as a little seed that transforms into a mighty oak, which is constantly moving its branches, its form, toward light. That is what we are geared to do. What has gone awry is our belief system; our thinking has misguided our life force toward darker forces. It's as if we have told the branch to grow toward the shade, not toward the light. It believes us, trusts us, and goes where we have told it. So my beliefs, my fears and concerns, about my children is my brilliant life force being misdirected, in this case toward fear. I have come to believe that fear is life-affirming and believe that worry is my life force—that it feeds, sustains, and nurtures life. It is challenging to realize this. Very challenging. Shocking to me because it seems so wrong. But I have watched myself do this. I see it in myself, I hear it. I see it in many others. It is at the core of so much of our lives; how we work, teach, exercise, treat illnesses, eat, and make love. It underlies everything we do; all aspects of our lives.

I go deeper into my meditation. I realize that I need the fear. The fearful thoughts produce fear in my body. A tenseness in my muscles; in the very fabric of my body. The chemical changes produce the tenseness, the hardening of my body. It's an all-encompassing process. It must effect every muscle, fiber, and cell of energy flow in my body. What I am radiating within me and what is radiating off of me. The visible and the invisible parts of me, vibrating with fear. And this is what we have been looking for: this tightness. This has been the goal. We have come to believe that this tightness is our source of security. That it provides protection and sustenance. That is what our life force wants—to be sustained, cared for, and nurtured. It is geared toward protection—to seek safety, security, and protection from dangerous forces. We are fully alive and our life force will do everything and anything to stay alive; to grow and to thrive. It is an amazing gift that comes along with the package of life. This ingrained, unrelenting drive to be alive. Our thinking—and it's hard to understand how it became so distorted over the ages—has come to believe that this feeling of fear, this whole-bodied life experience of fear, is a life-sustaining force. So we seek it out. We seek out this protective, sustaining force when we sense that we are in danger. It actually makes sense. It is very smart, powerful and pragmatic.

But here's the big catch: somehow we have come to associate danger with success. We have attached the danger label onto our life guidance system; onto stuff that is actually life-affirming—Health, happiness, joy, freedom, wealth, you name it. Somehow we have attached the label of danger, or destructive, to the very essence of life itself. Our life-sustaining mechanism has come to believe that real living is dangerous. And so, when we are doing well—really living—we will attack it. We will seek to defeat it in an attempt to protect ourselves, to keep ourselves alive. In our misguided brilliance, in the face of joy we will choose fear; we will choose to create tension and hardness in our beings. We will create a phase of insecurity as a way to counteract and defeat that which we have perceived as dangerous—life itself. That is amazing to witness.

5.2 Caught in the Act

We have caught it. It is amazing to catch this, to get a glimpse of us working. It's like catching a thief in the act of stealing. *Gotcha*. When this happens, it's a great act of grace. It's the moment when I get to see through the veil, the guise; when I see the real thing in action, I am blessed. I am on the road to freedom. The game may not be over, but I *gotcha*. This is a great relief to me.

Now we get to have a conversation. So I start talking to this part of me. This seat of genius. I may give her a name, or just start talking. I can introduce myself; say hello. Start a conversation. Often, I naturally say that I am sorry. Sorry for placing this false truth onto her. Imagine this was your child. Your most precious child. In actuality, this is even more precious than your child. It's the closest entity to you in life; it's You. Your most precious, pure self. I say that I am sorry because I have guided her away from her natural form. I have directed her away from doing what she was built, created, to do. She has been bred to go toward the light. But she has done what I have asked and grown toward the dark. And I am sorry. Really sorry for doing this. She is amazing. An amazing friend, ally, buddy, confidant. She will do what I ask of her. With great gusto, great allegiance; in the face of challenge, she will keep at it, patient, 100% committed to my direction, unwavering, confident, sure, singularly focused on me, on my direction. And I am sorry.

I was geared to play, to create, and to make beautiful things. That is my nature. It might be yours too. Light is where I thrive. It's my home. My Hebrew name is Avner: of light, keeper of light, shedder of light. Imagine what it would be like if someone asked me to stay still, to stay small, to not play, and be in the dark. It gets worse. Imagine that I loved this asker so much that I was willing to do it. I was happy to do it. What would be the ramifications of this? A player of light, sitting in the darkness. Not just for a moment or a day, but for decades. It became my way of being. How would you feel if you did that to someone you loved? Me, I feel really sorry; really sorry. Sorry isn't even enough. It's painful to consider. Painful to consider that I did this. Really painful to consider that I did this to myself. This is what I did to my brilliance. I told it to stay shut, to sit still, to stay in the dark. I had come to believe that the light, my play, my creativity, was dangerous, would put me in danger, would hurt me. So I told myself to stay still. You have done this too. You may be doing it right now.

What do you say to yourself? What do you say when you realize you have shut yourself down? What do you say when you realize you have imprisoned yourself. What do you say to yourself? I said, "I am sorry." It was the most natural thing to say. "I am sorry." And I really meant it. I am sorry.

> *I am an artist.*
>
> *I am brilliant.*
>
> *I am a brilliant artist.*
>
> *I am creative.*
>
> *I am very creative.*
>
> *I am alive.*
>
> *I love being alive.*
>
> *I love being alive.*
>
> *Alive.*

5.3 Talking with Brilliance

I spoke to myself, my brilliance, as if I was talking to another soul, another entity, another person. It was easier for me to do this. It felt separate, not a part of me, a separate entity. Hello, Brilliance, My name is Evan. It felt really good to talk to Brilliance in this way. It made her full, complete, strong, identifiable, alive, real. I quietly thought that I was really speaking to myself, but this was an important step, seeing brilliance, as an entity to herself.

> *I'm not sure. Is my Brilliance, a brilliance given to me, alive in me? Is Brilliance truly a separate entity, or is she me? I kind of like the idea of this entity.*

Brilliance is fully dedicated to me, running around in me, through my life. Doing her brilliance thing for me, in service of me. An actual brilliance, fully formed, custom designed for me and my life. Unleashed in me. She has friends too: Intelligence, Kindness, Ge-

nius, Patience, and a whole bunch more. All of them are alive. They
are their own entities, working brilliantly and patiently together. In
simpatico, coordinated, dedicated, together for me. Wow, what a
neat idea. I love it. Built in friends. Amazing friends, fully dedicated
to me, to life, to the divine purpose. Always on. Always present.
Available. Ready to go. Doing their thing. I love this idea.

I ask Brilliance to be brilliant, to take over, to do what she was born
to do. To do my giftedness, to bring my brilliance out fully. To be
brilliant and to use my brilliance to heal what has been misguided.
This is a great relief to me. To let go. To let her grow to the light, to
unleash her brilliance—her true brilliance.

5.4 Another Option

What if Brilliance, Patience, and Generosity are who I am?
What if I've been speaking to myself? Developing a relationship with *Me*. In saying, "hello, I'm sorry, can you help me?"
and "thank you" to myself, I am really speaking to me. What if I
am Brilliant? What if I am Patient? What if I am Generous? What
if I am saying sorry to myself? Not to a separate entity but to me.
What if I am speaking to my core, to me, precious me? What if I've
been apologizing to me?

"I am sorry," I am saying sorry to me. This would be an act of love.
"I am sorry." Realizing that I am brilliant, kind, and generous; this
too would be an act of love; of real love. Saying 'I love you' is saying
'I love me.' This is who I am. Recognizing who I truly am. What a
gift. What an act of love. Recognizing my own brilliance. My own
kindness. My own courage. 'I am loving. I am kind. I am brilliant.'

5.5 Jerry the Protector

I seek protection. Our need for protection is part of a wholesome
life. We need it. We have cells that protect us from other cells. We
have skin that protects us from foreign substances. We have emotional structures that protect us from harmful influences. Fences
make sense. I seek protection from natural disasters, from illnesses,

from negative thought patterns, from distracting beliefs. I seek protection from financial, emotional, and physical harm. Protection is a good thing to have.

For much of my life I have felt unprotected. I am sure that much of my fear stems from not feeling cared for. I had clothes, food, a house. I always had the stuff I needed. As I felt my life falling apart, as my fear began to gain traction over me, I sought help. I didn't understand what was happening. It was bewildering; out of the blue. Where did this come from? I felt very vulnerable. It's from this state that I started to seek. To try and understand. To find help. At the time, I did not understand what was happening to me. I felt raw; unprotected. I wasn't even sure where to turn for help. I had a family friend: Ben. He was a rabbi and had a therapy background. He was the first person I called. He seemed to understand and suggested I see a therapist. I called him right away. Therapy was my start. It wasn't enough. I needed something more. I thought of meditation, but that scared me. It wasn't familiar—foreign—and I wasn't sure I could trust that. I went with prayer. Yelling out prayers, literally. From my childhood I knew many of the Jewish prayers. I had a prayer book with me. It was very familiar to me. When I woke I would open my prayer book. I started saying the prayers out loud—very loudly, almost yelling them. I needed some way to get out of my head; to help with the fear thoughts and sensations I was experiencing. I wasn't thinking of God or salvation. The prayers worked because they gave me something to do. Something that I trusted. In hindsight, 30 years later, I believe I was actually calling out, working with, being helped by God, by the Godliness and holiness of these prayers. It wasn't on my mind at the time. I just needed something to do, something to throw myself into—a diversion, and one I trusted.

I wasn't thinking of protection at the time, nor the need for presence, generosity, caring or abundance. I was unaware of my need for sustenance; spiritual sustenance. I was unaware of it, but my body, my being, was seeking it out, seeking it out strongly. I knew, my big 'I' knew, what I needed. Brilliance knew. Thirty years later I have started to speak to Brilliance directly. I have realized my need for her. I am becoming aware of her presence, her availability, her *livingness* in me. It feels really good to call out to her. To ask her for help. To let her know that I'm aware of her. That I'm sorry for holding her back. Giving her my thumbs up. Go, do, take it on. Please. Thank you.

Thirty years later I'm becoming aware of my need for protection, for care, for guidance, for love. I decided to expand my Brilliance game. If there is Brilliance, Honesty, and Patience; there must be Protection. If there is built-in Brilliance, there must be built-in Protection. To make it easier for me to communicate with Protection, I gave him a name. Jerry. Jerry the Protector.

My Jerry has the full capacity to provide protection; in its most brilliant, complete, and divine form. Jerry is imbued with the same divine force that created and creates all life. He is full of the force that created gravity and trees; that allows a seed to turn into a flower, that creates neurons, history, and time itself. The knowledge that created all out of nothing. This same brilliance is in Jerry. Jerry the Protector is brilliant, possessing all the brilliance of creating. That is who Jerry is. We can take great confidence in Jerry. There is no lack or failing in Jerry. Not just brilliance but unwavering, completely loyal brilliance—won't flinch, won't get distracted, doesn't fail at all. Complete brilliance, perfect protection. Jerry the Brilliant Protector. This gives me great confidence and peace. If we need protection, clearly, Jerry is our man. I like playing with this idea. It gives me comfort. I don't know how true it is. I know I'd like it to be true. Maybe it is. My friend, Bob, tells me that the universe will give us evidence for everything we believe. When we choose to believe something, we will interpret our lives from that belief. My friend, Ralph, will interpret an event in a way so that it gives him the most peace of mind. Jerry the Protector. I'd like to play with him more. I'd like to feel a greater sense of faith, of protection and care. I'd like to feel a closer relationship to the divine. To feel guidance. To feel loved. Along with Brilliance, Jerry the Protector may be able to help me.

5.6 Do I Matter?

What changes when I give Protection a name? What happens when I identify my need for protection? What changes when I become aware that protection is a divine entity in me? What changes? Hasn't Jerry been here all along? Did Jerry need me? Does protection need me to claim and name him? What does my awareness change? What does my claiming change? This reminds me of prayer. It probably is a form of prayer. One of my favorite prayers is 'help me.' Another is 'thank you.' I pray in many many ways. Sometimes I consider each breath a prayer. I'm curious. If Jerry is already present, if Brilliance is already part of our life force, then what changes when we identify her, or call on her, or ask her for help? What is different? What impact does our praying have? What do our prayers do? Why does my participation matter? What does it matter when you pray for me? When we pray for others? When others pray for us?

5.7 Playing in the Band

Let's play with this a bit... ... Imagine Brilliance, Jerry the Protector, Patience, Love, and Creativity are all in a band: Hanging out; doing their thing. They really don't need me to call on them, to bring them out, to introduce them. They don't need me to be their producer. They are playing all the time. It's what they do. They also like it and respond when we call to them. Imagine being in school. You are walking down the hall. You see some buds hanging out and you call out to them. "Yo Mark," "Hey Stein," "Demeat," "Thorpie," and they look up. As you approach you may give each other a high five, maybe a hug. Acknowledgement and connection. You enter the conversation. Start to talk. The dynamic changes now that you are involved. You bring a certain energy to the group and they are sharing their energy with you. Individually and collectively. This will change again when another friend joins the crowd. They were there all along. You too were in the building. But something changes when you come together. When you acknowledge one another. When you start to talk. To relate. To be together.

I like the idea of unleashing. Of unleashing something that is already there. What if we unleash Brilliance and Jerry the Protector when we acknowledge them. We unleash them when we recognize their existence. We unleash them when we ask them for help. They are always here but we play a role in unleashing their capacity when we start to believe in them. When we start to believe in their power, we release them. They are set more free. Given more space to roam and work and do their thing through our lives. We give them more reign, more space, more freedom. I imagine they really like it when I let go. When I give up control and stop trying to direct them. I imagine they like it when they find out that I trust them. When I let go. 'Brilliance, I let go of trying to do your job.' 'I'm sorry for getting in your way.' 'Please, go do your thing.' I imagine they like this very much. I imagine they get excited; motivated. They can't wait to do their thing. To be unleashed, let go, let free to do their brilliance in me, through me. It's their job, what they were created to do. To do their fullest for us, for our lives, for our stories, our journeys. We are given the opportunity to acknowledge them. What if God gives us the freedom to choose them? To choose to trust them? To choose to let them do their thing? We are given this gift again—the gift of choice.

5.8 Tethered Angels

I've got to believe that beliefs, attitudes, habits, and assumptions can tether my angels. When I'm trying to control situations, I must be hampering them in some way. When I am impatient, this must have an impact on their influence. When I lack faith—if I'm dishonest or closed-minded—it must have an impact. In these moments I must be corralling them, limiting their space to roam freely, to work, to do their thing. I must be leashing them when I act against their nature. When I try to do their job. It feels like telling a dog to stay put: 'Don't move.' Like telling a child to 'sit still' when they really want to play. It's a form of putting someone down, criticizing them. It depletes. It sucks energy. It shuts down. To humans, it's hurtful. I walk away feeling deflated. Rejection.

My guess is that they don't feel this way. They probably don't take it personally. But I'm sure there is an impact. Maybe not on them, but on us. We end up less inflated, more limited, more restrained. We inhibit their full impact; we block their power, their influence. Thank God they are divine. They will do their best to keep us alive in spite of our resistance, neglect, rejection. They are loyal, unflappable. We may have limited their capacity but they keep coming any way.

5.9 Grace at Work

I'm thinking that this is Grace at work. This is her role. She swims among them all. Their cheerleader, director, guide. Her job is to keep them going. Working on our behalf even when we try to limit them. When the time comes, when we reach out, seek, invoke, and call on them, she sends them forth, directs them to us more fully, in the right time, in the right amount, in the right ways. "Go," she says to them, "Go, do your thing." "The party is on." "We are welcome here." "Go for it."

5.10 Best Buds

Gravity. The Wright brothers could not get us flying without gravity. The same force that keeps us planted on the earth became a playmate of flight. Brilliance must be the same. As we acknowledge her, we are freed up to use her. Magical things start to happen. We free up our divine qualities; free them to work their magic on and through us. We get to start playing with them. Just like a new playmate. As we get to know each other, we start to play. We start to create new games and expand each other's capacity to explore, discover, and learn. We do new stuff. Meet new folks. Play more. Find new ways of thinking. Meet new people.

Brilliance, Jerry, and Patience are amazing playmates. They love us. They are totally loyal. That too is built into them. They are proud of us and believe in us. They bring us gifts. Introduce us to their friends. All the things that great friends do for one another. They love it when we befriend them. It is a great gift to these folks. Our unleashing of them might be the greatest gift we can give them. It's our way of being their friend. They love it. They love when we play with them, when we acknowledge them, ask for their help, give them free reign. It gets them excited, gives them energy and unleashes their power, their brilliance. I like this idea. I like it a lot.

5.11 Freedom to Find 'It'

I can talk to Brilliance, the entity in me, and I can see myself as brilliant. Both of these ideas bring me more peace and confidence. Some days I find it easier to talk directly to Brilliance. Sometimes I get more comfort when I realize I am brilliant. But here's the bigger picture: Finding beliefs, actions, and concepts that bring us peace and confidence that allow us to see ourselves in a better light, that give us more faith. You may find *it* in a tree. In a rosary? In God. In a higher power. In a church, ashram, basketball court, or a fire pit. In a drum. In a support group. Maybe you chant or listen to Bruce. Yoga, Jazzercize. In a journal. Maybe it doesn't really matter where we find *it*, just as long as we do. The freedom to find it in any way that works for us. Our freedom to find it! May you find *it* now.

5.12 Built-in Protection

What if I don't really need protection? At least not in the idea of some external, masterful force that gives me protection; like a chaperone, or bodyguard, or benevolent powerhouse. What if Jerry is not outside of me, not an external force? What if it's even better? What if our security, our protector, is built into life and comes along with the deal? What if it's fully part of what we get with this life thing and God has built it right from the start? Not as an extra, an add-on, or bonus, but right from the start, as an essential ingredient of life. Protection. Imagine that Jerry comes along for the ride. Not only are we given life, we are given this instant protection too. It gets even better because this would mean that it is safe to live. We are safe. We are living in a fully-padded environment. Only safety surrounds us. Wow, this is mind-blowing to me. I am safe? I am safe? I am always safe? I am someone who has lived with such fear and a deep register of insecurity. I am the guy who used to wake up with one main goal: making it through the day without stepping on a mine. I was sure that life was unsafe, full of dangerous stuff just waiting to get me. The idea of built-in security is amazing. Revolutionary. No gaps? No space to fall? Are you telling me that we are safe? Safe because there is no unsafe? We don't need protection? Protection from what? If it is all safe, then there is no need for protection—all safe, all safe, all safe. What if we believed that it was all safe? What would it mean for you? What would it mean if you believed that it was all safe? If you believed that you and your children were safe? What could that mean?

5.13 Them Too

If I knew that I was safe, that safety was built into life, what else might I know? Could it mean that peace, fulfillment, and plenty are built in too? What if our lives were naturally fertile, alive, and radiant? If we are always thriving? What an amazing gift! Not only are we brought to life, but to a life that is truly alive, full, and plentiful.

5.14 What about the Pain?

There are times when we are in pain; sometimes in real pain. How can this possibly fit into a belief of *built-in safety, peace, and plenty*? What about when we are hungry, struggling financially, or in a place of real lack? What do we do with being attacked, hurt, bullied, abused, and badly mistreated? How about when we are afraid, in emotional pain, feeling lost? There are many, many people on the planet in dire need; under very harsh conditions. How can there be built-in protection when we are suffering?

This is an important question. It is vital.

Where is our hope, faith, and trust when we are going through the difficult times of life; through the hardest of times? Where is our peace? Where is God in these spaces? When I'm going through pain, I feel alienated, separated from, alone, unattended to. I feel like I'm off. I should be somewhere else. I should be over there; in the okay zone. Not in this pain situation. There is a gap: A gap between where I am and where I am supposed to be.

This makes the pain situation worse.

It takes great work—mental and faith work—to find acceptance. To find some way to believe that this situation of pain, of lack; is part of my Godly life. To see that the protection, the care, the thriving are in gear even when I'm in pain.

It doesn't make sense. Why would God create life; create me in such a way that I would be in this situation? In this pain? In these periods, it feels like God is lacking. Like I am lacking. Like I am not enough. If everything were okay, I wouldn't be here. I'd be over there. Life is much easier to live when we are at peace, when everything is okay. It's downright hard when in lack: When we are in emotional pain, or physical pain, suffering, or in the many forms of financial, emotional, and spiritual need. It's really hard. It is natural to feel alienated from the divine—divine care, divine love, divine protection. How could I be protected or cared for in this situation? It takes a lot of work to see it, to believe it, to trust it. But get this: it helps. Is it better to go through your pain with the added pain of feeling spiritually alone and uncared for? What changes in your body, in your mind, in your spirit when you decide, when you choose to decide, that yes, I am being cared for. Even in this shit place, I am being cared for. What would it change on a cellular level if you believed that you were being guided, that you were being protected and nourished, even during this pain. What if you believed that this pain was a gift? A gift of spiritual growth and nourishment. What if you went so far as to believe that you chose this? You chose this in love. Not in some form of sadistic pain giving, but as a form of love for yourself; a form of recalibration.

Every pain situation I have been through has brought me closer to me, to my authentic self. It has brought me to spirit; more deeply and expansively and authentically to my spirit, to my spiritual life. It has helped me to find healthier ways to live, to express myself, to feel connected to my divine; to God directly. My whole spiritual life was cracked open by pain and suffering, by deep loneliness and fear. You've gone through your versions of this too. Some of us more than others. It may show up as physical disease, an ailment, an accident. It may show up in financial loss, or in personal losses of all kinds. It may show up in the forms of mental disease, addictions, and break downs of all sorts. And they may last for moments or decades. It may be at the hands of another's attack; the result of very harsh desperate situations or of deep, deep loss. The kinds you don't think you can get through. It may take the form of deep, deep pain. The really deep stuff. It may take any or all of these forms. It may be very painful, very scary. You may not even survive it in human form. Where is the built-in protection, built-in abundance, care, love, thriving in this pain? What if you chose to believe it was still there? What would change if you believed it was? What would change if you believed? What would change? What would change if you knew God was here too—loving you, right here, in this pain. What would change?

This may be the most important work we do in our lifetimes—discovering that divine protection and love are here too.

5.15 Pissed Off

I was so pissed off at God.

He brought me to life, then put me into a game of threat, of fear, of being tested, of suffering, of pain. What kind of bullshit is that? Who would bring someone to life and then throw them into a prison, full of torture, with rules that don't make sense; full of failure and pain. Hopes that got smashed and evidence—plenty of evidence—of pain and misfortune. That is how I lived much of my young adult life—pissed off at God.

I didn't yet realize I was doing it to myself.

5.16 Fear Reactions

Do you know how much fear influences the way we speak, the way we act, the decisions we make? It gets better. You deal with people who are doing the same: speaking, acting, reacting out of fear. It's actually pretty funny, like a sit-com. You are reacting to their fear—which is triggered by your fear, which, in turn, stimulates their reactions—and leads to more fear. Fear stimulating fear, causing more fear and insecurity, causing more fear. It's amazing we get anything done.

Have you ever talked to an ex-bully? It has been so surprising to me. I was always scared of confrontation, of being beaten up by tough guys; bullies. These guys were amazing to me. They didn't seem afraid of the confrontation. This made them even scarier to me. I could not have been more wrong. Go talk to one of these folks. Guess what you'll hear? They were scared to death, just like me—maybe even more scared. Maybe you ran or sulked or got small in fear, but not these guys. Their reaction to fear was to lash out, to fight, to get aggressive. It was shocking for me to hear. Their reaction may have been different from mine, but the fear was there too. I felt relieved, like less of a wuss. I didn't feel so *not good enough* anymore. I wasn't such a loser for feeling afraid, for running from a fight, for being afraid of confrontation. Can anger be far behind? When angry, you may yell, get aggressive, get in someone's face. Maybe you get controlling or passive aggressive. Maybe you run away. That is your way of being angry. Sabotage? Putting someone else down? Pouting? Sulking?

This isn't just for individuals. Individuals make up families, organizations, businesses, and societies. Each of these individuals come with their own fear reactions, their anger responses. These systems containing many people turn into one big game. One big give and take of anger and fear. A giant stew of fear and anger. It really is amazing that we get stuff done—that real positive stuff gets done even with all this fear and anger going on. Imagine what we could do if we didn't react this way? Imagine what we could do? Imagine what we could do? Imagine?

What if I told you I was afraid? What if I could tell you that I felt intimidated? What if I didn't have to run away? What if you didn't have to lash out at me. Imagine what we could do? This isn't just two people in an interaction. These are families, groups of people, organizations, countries, cultures—all intermingling. All reacting to one another. Imagine if we could tell each other how afraid we were. What if we could tell each other how angry we felt? If we could do this, then we could start to tell each other how much we needed one another. I can ask you for help. I can start to trust you. I can tell you that I love you. I can actually love you. I can act in loving ways. It's built into us, these loving ways, nourishing ways, caring ways. It's built into us. Built into us individually and built into us communally, societally, humanly. Can you imagine what could be possible?

When I am enough—even a little enough—then I can tell you I'm afraid. If I sense that you have some *enoughness*, then I can tell you. We can start to love and care for each other more. We won't have to run away as much, won't have to control as much, won't have to manipulate as much. When I know you are enough. When I know that I'm enough. We become enough. We become enough. We become enough. We can say, "I am afraid". "I am scared." "I am angry." "Can you help me?"

Can you imagine?

5.17 Sharing Our Hopes Too, Beyond Our Fears

I am happy. I am working on a really neat project. Do you want to hear what I'm working on? I really want to go to Europe. I'm thinking of starting a company. Can we talk about how we are communicating? I am writing a book. I want to be rich. I'd like to be an artist, a photographer. I'm thinking about sailing around the globe. I'd like to start rock climbing. Do you want to go to the movies with me?

Can you imagine?

5.18 Taking it Communally

How can we live here together? Can we use some of your land? We like your rituals. We are running low on water. Do you have grain to share? If you can loan us $1,000 we could start this project. What if our beliefs collide? Can we find a way to work together? I'm not sure what you mean.

Can you imagine?

5.19 Taking it Globally

How can we be safe? We are afraid of your power. We are afraid of your bombs. We need more resources. We need more security. We are feeling alone. We have dreams for our people. We want to thrive, too. How do we get more of what you have? We feel less than. We feel left behind. We feel isolated. We think this land belongs to us.

5.20 More Grace

Can you imagine a power so beautiful and loving that it can cut through our mirage of fear—cut through our addiction to struggle? Can you imagine that something sustains us even in the face of our attempt to sabotage? Grace; it has to be. How else do we explain the great things we do accomplish? In the face of all this fear, we still accomplish so much good. We experience so much good. It has to be grace: Saving grace, plentiful grace, nourishing grace, joyous grace, fun grace, caring grace, loving grace, sustaining grace, patient grace, innovative grace, making-up-for-our-mistakes grace, life grace.

5.21 Fear Here Too?

Alive. Organizations. Alive.

Organizations touch other organizations; alive things touch other alive things. Families, countries, communities, cells in our bodies; all interacting with one another. The same fear dynamic exists between organizations, between living things. One's fear touching another's fear—responding in fear, responding back in fear. On and on and on and on. Fear feeding fear. I really wonder: War, slavery, hunger, hoarding of resources, poverty, famine, disease. Is fear at work here too? I wonder.

5.22 Do We Need It?

I wonder. Do we need fear? Do we need it to protect ourselves? To sustain our life? It seems like we are building a world-wide, life culture built on fear. How fucked up is that? Do we need it? The fear, poverty, hunger, hoarding? Do we think we need it to protect ourselves? Is it possible that these too are manifestations of struggle, of our need for struggle? Could these be manifestations of *not good enough*? Could these be manifestations of our *not good enough* too?

5.23 How the Hell?

We are divine. How the hell are we letting fear create so much?

5.24 World-Wide Grace

Society grace, community grace, history grace, culture grace, world-wide grace. Has to be—don't you think? How else to explain it? Grace. A whole lot of Grace. World-Wide Grace. Even better: Universal Grace. Universal Grace. Full Blown Universal Grace. What the heck? Grace. Pure. Complete. Grace.

5.25 Love Economy: *OTS = OLS*

Many people are helped by our attempts to fight hunger, disease, and war. But here's the big problem: we will continue to create it in other areas, with other people, populations—or worse, back with the same folks we've already helped. These efforts are important and valiant but they will not last until we address the underlying cause—enough. The same is true for individuals. We will continue to find forms of struggle until we come to realize we are enough. Until we realize we are loved. We as individuals, families, businesses, organizations of all sizes, communities, countries, peoples, our whole planet. We need to find love. Real love. To find out that we are loved, that we are enough, that we have enough, do enough. We need to find divine love. We truly need to find love in ourselves and love ourselves. These are probably one and the same—divine love/loving ourselves.

Maybe you find these words too trivial or weak or not enough, too pie-in-the-sky, too sentimental. Heck, they scare me because I'm not sure I believe them. I think I do. In a very practical way, they make sense to me. Real. Powerful. Pragmatic. Important. Impactful. Result Driven. Our *enough* quotient. Our *love* quotient underlies everything we do, every thought we have, every action we take. Everything. And it is free of charge. This may be one of its biggest selling points.

Organizations, companies, entrepreneurs of all shapes and sizes don't think they can make money off love. They feed so much off disease, anger, and fear. I would love to do an economic evaluation to determine how much of our world economy is based on fear. To see the economic impact of fear on healthcare, law enforcement, the military, the foods we eat, our security systems, education. All of it. Is there any area of our economy that isn't impacted? No way.

We have a whole economic system deeply built on fear.

All of it. Can you imagine the economy of fear? How big and self-sustaining is it? We need not be afraid of all we will lose. The wealthy don't have to lose their wealth. As we come to more love, this too will generate an economy. It has too. There will be more, much more for all.

Our fear economy is built on assumption. An assumption of limited supply. The assumption that there is some limited supply of things we need: That we need to grapple over, hoard, and protect this limited supply. But what if that is not true? What if there is unlimited supply? What if the supply will always increase? What if we can never run out?

The *stuff* is just a distraction. The real supply is love. God's love. That is the real supply. That is the magical force behind our stuff. Love. Here's something to consider: What if our stuff, our amount of stuff is based on our assumption of our amount of love? A mathematical formula. Einstein-like. Our tangible stuff is equal to our assumption about how much love stuff we have. Our stuff, our tangible stuff, is based on our love stuff. To the extent that we feel loved. To the extent that we believe we are loved. Our supply of stuff will equal the amount of love stuff we have. Limited supply is based on limited love. Our belief in the amount of love.

> *Our Tangible Stuff = Our Love Stuff*
>
> $OTS = OLS$

Divine love is unlimited. We may not believe it or feel it; but it has to be. Divine love has to be unlimited. We are enough by the shear fact that we are alive. We are loved the same. We are loved. That is our nature. Our divine nature as divine creations. We are loved. We are loved by a universal, unlimited, limitless, divine source. Unlimited love. Unlimited supply. Unlimited love, unlimited supply.

Therefore, our OTS is actually unlimited.

5.26 Unlimited Supply

God, our universe is unlimited. It will continue to supply and feed us. What if that was the belief that we were living on? Imagine this belief stood at the foundation of our economy. Unlimited divine love and care.

5.27 E = E

Our *enoughness* is based on our *enoughness*. Our *enoughness*—our sense that we are enough, that we are good enough—will equal our sense of *enoughness*—as in having enough. Not only our sense, but also our actual tangible stuff. Our stuff will be enough based on our sense of our *enoughness*. As our *enoughness* quotient increases, so does our actual *enoughness*. This may be perceptual as in, "I feel, I believe that I have enough." "As I am enough, I have enough." But it may be bigger. As we personally and societally believe we have enough, our *enoughness*, our tangible *enoughness*, will grow. As in food supply, healthfulness, education, housing. All of our stuff. Fun stuff, fuel stuff, clothing stuff, transportation, land, air, water, innovation. All of our stuff. It will all increase to the extent we believe and know we are enough.

5.28 Soaring

It is easier to be generous when we come from *enough*. Our creativity soars, our solutions, our resolutions. The *enough* we are talking about is the *divine enough*, the *enough* that created the whole life system out of nothing. Like gravity, molecules, DNA, universes, all the stars. All of it. The stuff we have discovered and all the stuff we have yet to find out about. Love—this love, the source of our *enoughness*—has been the creator of it all. Can you imagine what could happen if we got with that love force? The creative genius behind everything that has ever been created. The first tool, fire, the wheel, electricity, law, literature. Everything. Everything that has been and is yet to come. Imagine it unleashed. Imagine this power unleashed, unencumbered by our fear. Unencumbered.

Untethered. Our fear cannot stop it—never has. Grace is too strong to let that happen. Our fear slows it down, slows us down, creates the struggle; but it can't stop it. Can't stop love. Fear cannot stop love. Slows it down, gets in its way. Can't stop it. Imagine what could be possible. Imagine it. An economy of love. Unleashed. Love unleashed. Magnificent. Absolutely magnificent.

5.29 More Grace

Grace, is here, permeating through the veil, through the fear, anger, misbeliefs, the many manifestations of our fear. Through it all we still live, we get better, we don't completely destroy ourselves, and we thrive. How is that possible? Because the love has grace in it. It can maneuver around, get through the cracks. It is unstoppable. It will keep us alive in the face of our attempts to die.

5.30 Dying to Live

To keep ourselves alive and safe, we will attempt to die to do it. This is the biggest lie of the whole struggle/fear/not enough system. This is the essence of addiction. We come to believe that dying is the safest way to live. Nuts, right? Insanity? Absolutely!

6

Creation in Enough

6.1 Are They True? Does it Matter?

It feels really good to write; when I can let ideas flow through me and share them. Often when I write, I am the reader too. A witness. A witness to new ideas. I am a reader. Reading, witnessing ideas coming through me. Sometimes it's concepts I have thought about before, but often it's new ideas. Fantastic ideas. Sometimes I love them. As a reader I feel a *wow* inside, and think, 'what a neat idea.' Sometimes I feel excited because the idea is new. It makes a lot of sense to me and seems smart, really smart. New. Wow. Exciting to read them. To think them.

But often I'm afraid to write them down. Are they true? What will others think? Can I live up to them? Will others expect me to live up to them? But they make sense and they actually feel good. They seem truth-filled. Are they true? I'm not sure. They sound right, they make sense, they're new. These words have flowed right out and through me.

6.2 No Other

I am painting our office wall. I am cutting in the paint between the wall color and the ceiling. In that moment, the ceiling is the enemy, opposing me. I'm not wanting to get paint on the ceiling. But what if we are all in this together—me, the paint, the brush, and the ceiling? Then there is no opposition. All of us are in it together. We all desire success. There is no other outcome. The other possibility might be paint on the ceiling. Against, opposing my goal of a clean demarcation between wall and ceiling colors. No treading over = success. Paint on the ceiling = failure. What if we are all in this as one? What if there is no possible defeat—no other, no opposition, no failure? You may think that means no paint on the ceiling, but that might be impossible; or difficult. Either way, it limits the definition of the possibilities of success.

6.3 Conversations

I know these ideas are not unique. They emanate out from many places. I'm not always sure where they come from. I know that many ideas come from conversations. Many, many conversations I have had. Many people I have listened to. Their spoken voices and their written voices. There are many influences coming through. It's really cool when they do—and exciting. It gives me comfort to know that I am not just making this stuff up.

6.4 Fear Voices

For most of my life I have been afraid to speak and write what I honestly believe. My fear voices tell me that retribution will come if I do this. For many years I did not actually hear these voices or know they were influencing me. If you told me I was afraid to let myself out, I would have denied it. I had very little clue of what I was up to, or not up to. As I have become more aware, I have become more aware of this fear. Fear of getting beat up, fear of bad stuff happening to my children. Fear of being persecuted, tortured, jailed, killed, or hurt in some way. I justify it by looking at aspects of history. 'See, look at all these people and peoples who have and who are being hurt for their beliefs. For speaking their beliefs.'

These are some of the ways that my fear voices come at me. They sound so real when I hear them. It's hard to get some distance from the voices, from the possibility of them. I believe them. And that is where their power comes from. I believe them. Then I act on that belief or not act because of that belief. These actions in fear and inaction of fear multiply add up, create results, create habits, create consistent patterns of being. Create my life. A life created by fear.

6.5 Harbingers of Good

These voices started chirping two minutes after writing this section. I should probably take them as a harbinger of something very right. Why else would they come? But they scare me a bit. They are smart. They are built on pieces of truth—they use pieces of real evidence. I'm afraid my back will go out on me, I'll get sick, anxiety will kick in. All of these have happened before. My fear knows this. It uses pieces of evidence to build a case for itself. "See, I told you so."

They seem to come when something good is happening. When I'm breaking through for more freedom. More freedom. More growth. This is when they come—for protection. They say 'don't go there.' They are doing their job, protecting us. They believe that our destination is unsafe. We have taught them this. Our parents have taught us. So have teachers, movies, literature. So they come. Aha. We got it. Now we know. They must be harbingers. They must be harbingers of good, of growth, of freedom. Here's a way to fight back: claim something new. To claim that these fear voices are proof, evidence that we are on a right track. A new track. In a weird way, they are encouraging us to move forward. Letting us know everything is safe. In their own weird way, they are harbingers. Harbingers of good. In their own language, they are speaking clearly. Very clearly. Go. Go. Go forward.

6.6 Love Ourselves: A Pat on the Back

What happens when I am looking outward to feel better about myself? It is a dangerous move. I am looking to another to do what only I can give myself. What I really want is my own sense of *rightness*; my *ok-ness*. This is what I really desire. I have needed others to help me learn how to love myself and at some point I need to give that love to myself. My friends give me an awesome gift; they help me get to a point where I can give love to myself. That is the real goal; my ability to love myself. It is a sacred gift we seek and a sacred gift we earn; our ability to love ourselves. To give ourselves a pat on the back, to give ourselves a hug, to love ourselves. To love ourselves may be the greatest achievement we can accomplish in our life time. Ralph once told me that once he learned to love himself, then he was able to truly love others. I believe this although I'm not sure I understand it. I have not had that experience yet. Although as I am coming to love myself more, I do find that I am more forgiving and more understanding toward other people. I find that I want to do things that give them pleasure or make them feel more comfortable. I find that I am less critical. I am becoming more encouraging. I am more genuine and more heartfelt. I recently made a list of the ways I want Tara and be toward me. As I wrote the list, it dawned on me that I need to treat her these ways: encouraging, thoughtful, supportive, happy to see me, free to make mistakes, fun to be with, encouraging of my creativity. Ralphs' suggestion seems to describe a formula: Love of self is in direct to proportion to love of others.

Love of Self = Love of Others.

I don't completely understand the formula, but it sure makes sense to me.

Let's see if an analogy would help.

Until I actually have something, I can't give it away. If I wanted to give you my frog, I'd have to have my frog first. That seems pretty simple. Let's try this again. Can I give you *a* rock, if I don't have it first? I could point to a rock and you could pick it up. Then you would have a rock. But for me to *give* you a rock, do I need to *have* it? Let's try this on Love. Do I have to have the love in order to give it? Following our rock story, I guess I can show you love and I can act loving without actually having it. If this is so, then what is the difference between giving love and showing or acting love?

Let's think of an actor in a play depicting the life of a real person. They can perform the role and the lines. Their performance can touch me and I will feel real emotion. Now let's imagine the real thing; the actual person living the experience. One is a replica; one is the real thing. If I watched a play about two people loving each other, but it is not the experience of two people loving each other. The quality of the real life experience is quite different than the one evoked by a performance. This does not mean that people are in-sincere when they show us love but just that the quality of that love has got to be different than when we are actually giving someone our love—love that we have.

Is it possible to have love without having love for yourself. I've got to believe that genuine love does not have direction. It is simple love. If I have love then I have love of self. If I have love then I have love of others. What if love is love. Just like water is water. Love is love. If I have love I am loving. I am loving to you and I am loving to me. I am simply loving. How does this jive with the idea that once I can love myself then I can love you. Maybe I need to take the pronoun out of the picture. Once I love I love myself, love you, I love.

I know I can and have been caring toward other people even when I wasn't feeling much love for myself, but maybe I was missing something. Maybe I thought it was real caring or real love. Maybe I haven't truly loved others because I haven't truly loved myself; because I'm still learning, still gaining love. Maybe I'm more love that I was and that I can become even more love. What if I'll know it when I know it? I'm going to believe that this is the greatest gift

I can give or earn or develop in life. It sounds right to me. It just sounds right. If peace of mind, if happiness, if vitality and prosperity all emanate from this love, then it surely sounds like the greatest achievement I could have.

6.7 Stop

So I stopped and reminded myself of Brilliance. Of my brilliance. Of grace and brilliance. So I gave it to them. I gave this writing to them. Heck, it came from them. I gave it to them. I reminded myself of Ralph's words: God is protecting us. I gave the fear voice to Brilliance. She loves that. It's another chance to heal. Give it to them. Not only will Brilliance heal my fear of stepping forward—of telling truth and being my truth—it also allows the brilliant to shine forth. It does both at the same time. Heals the wound and brings light. Just like a flashlight in a dark room. The light lights up the room and rids it of darkness all in the same action. So I gave it over to Brilliance. I told Tara about it. I was taught that when we speak our fears to another, they lose their strength. I'll probably tell one of my friends too. This too will loosen the grip; help me see the insanity of my thinking. Break the spell of fear. I will continue to pray too: Seeking guidance, trusting the light, trusting brilliance, trusting the love force. This is where these ideas come from. They have come now for a reason. I can trust that too. Then I felt gratitude. Gratitude for receiving this knowledge and for the opportunity to write it down and share it with others. Gratitude for the clarity I receive in my ideas. While they come through my fingers, I feel like a reader, getting the information, getting the clarity. This is exciting. Rewarding. It feels good to speak a truth, to make an impact, to shed some light. I have helped myself so I am sure that others will be helped too. What the heck, this could make a really big impact. That is cool.

7

Enough with Others

7.1 Never Alone

I tried to be alone. I thought that if I could go a year without any contact with the people in my life, then I'd be okay. No contact with anyone that I knew. No one that I had a close relationship with. My parents. My brothers. All family. All friends. People I had worked with. If only I could go a year without any contact, then I would be okay. I would be healed. It didn't work. Just because I didn't see or talk to them didn't mean that I was alone. They were still here. In my life; in me. Their voices, their influences, their imprints on my life were still there. Running away was not a way to heal. It got worse actually. Their voices, their influences became magnified, got stronger. I was never really alone. Along with these folks who I believed had a negative influence on me, there was another aspect that I wasn't even aware of. I was surrounded by angels, ones that were alive, in flesh and blood. They were around me. Praying for me, caring for me, available to me. There were and are angels that I'd call *deadalive*. They had passed away in their physical form but were still around me, helping me, caring for me; even if I didn't see or acknowledge their existence. Tara recently heard a teacher share that we are surrounded at all times by an army of helpers. I did not consider them in my life at this time. But they were there and they still are now. They were around me all the time. I didn't even realize that my dog, Steamer, was an angel. That God has sent him to me and that he stayed with me until it was ok to leave until I was in a healthy enough place along my journey that it was ok for him to move on. And he still is in my life to this today. I often talk to him, ask him for help and connect to him. But even this isn't the whole truth. Does that mean he is not there but only when I reach out to him? My belief and experience tells me that these forces, our angels are with us all the time. I may not be aware of their presence and I may not actively reach out or communicate with them but that does not mean that they are not here.

Then there is source God, our creator. In my belief, s/he is with me all the time. Again I may not be aware of the presence and I may not choose to communicate directly with them but that doesn't mean they are not here. I am never alone, never alone. I tried so hard to get alone to get away from everyone. I thought that this would heal me. But it was only bringing me closer to my death. It is impossible to be alone and be alive. Impossible. So my attempt to extricate myself from everyone was actually me trying to rip myself away from life. Imagine trying to remove yourself from your breath. The only way I can see doing this is by holding my breath. What would actually happen if I tried to hold my breath? Eventually it just gets more painful. We are built to breathe. Eventually we have to breathe. Our impulse takes over and we breathe. My attempt to be alone was the same. This is quite different than getting time alone in a healthy way. Even in our breathing we need to let air out before we can breathe in again. It is a normal and healthy flow of energy. Being by myself is very important to me but in this case, I was trying to remove myself from life. It was impossible. Like a

breath held way too long, it just got more and more painful. My
desire to live was imposing itself. Like the invisible angels around
me, I couldn't see it. I just felt pain. It just got more and more painful. Little did I know that this pain was my life force attempting
to save me. I just kept recoiling, going deeper into my isolation in
an attempt to heal that pain. The strategy I was using to heal was
actually killing me. This is addiction at its finest. We get caught in a
strategy for living that is actually killing us.

7.2 Grace

I was sitting on my chair: In a lot of emotional pain, alone, afraid.
This had been going on, every day, for a long time; many months.
On this day something very significant was about to change. But
why on this day? I was in the same situation. This day was no different. I was laying in the chair watching TV; all day, as I did every
day. On this day I didn't do a special ritual. I didn't invoke certain
words or pray in a special manner. Often I think that God will only
help me if I pray right or do some ritual just right; in order to get
a real result, we have to figure out the right ritual and then do it
right; like a guarantee, or a divine recipe; this is how I was taught;
many of us pick up this belief. But on this day, the only ritual I did
was me being me, stuck in a chair, in a lot of pain. Then out of the
blue a series of thoughts came to me that would trigger a reaction,
an experience; that would change my life.

When I started my path of disconnecting from my life, a mantra
came to me one day.

> *I can't do anything until I do nothing.*

It hit me so strongly; sounded so profound. It validated the path
I was about to take. It was scary taking this step to leave all the
people in my life. It felt really real. Real implications. Not a short
vacation. It seemed that this action could and would cause life
implications. It would permanently impact the relations in my life.
At the same time I felt that I needed to do it to save my life. To save

my life. That is why I was doing this. I was lost. I felt trapped in patterns of relationships, in patterns of living that I could not get out of as long as I was involved with the people I was closest to. When I was with them, I would react, fall into a role that was not really me. It was a role that I came to play. I had to find out who I was. Who was I aside from the roles I played with these folks. I needed to purge myself, to get to the essence of myself. To remove myself from these influences so that I could find out what was there, what was my essence. When I heard this phrase in my mind, "I can't do anything, until I do nothing" I jumped on it. It was a savior. It told me what I was doing was not only correct, it was a spiritually true truth. I can't really do anything in my life, achieve my purpose until I get to a point of doing nothing. I sounded so right. It was a phrase I often came back as my pain and fear grew. In the face of what I was facing I would tell myself, 'I can't do anything until I do nothing.' It made me feel special; actually think I was on a special form of a spiritual trip. What I felt was fear, doubt, and loneliness. So on this day, I was laying in my chair as I did every day, all day. On this day, at that moment, a new thought came to me. How far would I go doing nothing? When I thought of losing my apartment. I realized that I would seek food and shelter in a shelter. In that moment I realized this wasn't nothing. By going to the shelter I was trying something. Then I thought of leaving of being out of the shelter, I would try to find food. Well this wasn't nothing either. It was an attempt to do something to fortify myself. So I went another step. All this going through my mind. Step by step, a logical progression as I lay in my chair. What was different about today? It wasn't a special day on the calendar. I didn't make a decision to have a special day. I didn't do a special incantation. I didn't call someone as ask them for a strategy to help myself. I didn't shoot up a special prayer. Why did I go through this process on this day?

What was about to happen was one of the most significant, important, and critical moments of my life. It sure didn't feel like a gift, but it was. I was about to hit bottom and it truly is one the greatest things that ever happened in my life. An act of grace that saved my life and I have no explanation for why it happened, how it happened, or why it happened at that moment.

As I realized that begging for food or getting it out of a *dumpster* wasn't nothing: I went another step. If I even lost this amount and it was cold I would probably try to lay on a steam grate for warmth. I realized this too was something. I was trying to better myself. And then it hit me. A question. How far would I have to go to do nothing?

Bam. I was about to have a very powerful moment of clarity. I have been taught that these moments of clarity are a gift. People call it Grace. Here was the clarity that hit me. My grace moment.

I realized that the finale of this game was my death. This game wanted me dead. To win this game there was only one option: death. The nothing I was looking for would only be achieved in one way. Death. My death. It was a shocking realization. I had no idea this was the game I was playing. Like the angels around me, this too I had been unware of. I had been traveling down a path with gusto. I thought the path was one of healing and emancipation. It was so shocking that the purpose of this game was the complete opposite. It would have been emancipating in a certain way. It would free me from living, but I thought this was a path to living more freely, happily, and joyously. It all happened so quickly. At that moment I literally raised my hands over my head. "I'm done." In that moment I spoke; to whom or what I'm not sure. I'm not sure if I spoke out loud or within my own head. I realized that this trip I was on was not one toward spiritual freedom; I was on a trip of death. I felt a bit like a chump. I was so close to winning. I could see an image in my head. It was like a scale, a ladder, a shaft. I could see how far I had come. I was so close to the *nothing* I was trying to achieve: the end. I was so close to winning this game. In that moment it hit me. These stakes were way too high. I was scared. I said, "I'm done. These stakes are too high for me." I didn't realize it, but in that moment I decided that I wanted to live. I didn't want to die. I didn't know that I wanted to live. I did know that I didn't want to die. That moment started my new life. A path I have been on since then. Trust me, everything didn't magically change that moment and yet in that moment everything did change. I cannot take credit for that moment. It felt like it happened to me. To me it is grace. God's grace. Life's grace. Grace. Pure grace.

For me Grace isn't something I can set in motion: Not something I can control. It is a gift. A gift whose timing and form are beyond my control. To me it is God's great act of love. Grace. A great act of love. For me, Grace is an act of love, given to me by the same force that created and creates life itself. THE creator helped me in that moment on that day. I can't tell you why then; why me. But I am so grateful. Without that bottom, without that grace, I don't think I would have the energy and drive to continue along my road to recovery; my road to living a full, loving, and joyous life.

Thank God that Grace is stronger than all our fear.

How else can you explain that we are alive and thriving, on this planet? Do I think I'm doing it?

Achieving results; making stuff happen.

Arrogance.

God is the creator, Grace is her gift to us.

All forms of our creation; GRACE.

Your creativity, your breath, your luck, your ideas, your great accomplishments.

Grace.

Grace in action.

Love in action.

Our creator's very personal love in action.

Loving me, loving you.

Loving all of us.

Love in action.

Grace.

8

Seeing

8.1 Seeing 1

I thought that seeing occurred with my eyes. I've learned that seeing happens in my mind. Seeing is a choice. It's an act of perspective: Of choosing perspective. Seeing is perspective choosing. I like that. Seeing is perspective choosing. Choosing perspective. Seeing is choosing perspective. Choosing perspective. That is what seeing is. Choosing perspective. Wow. Love that. Choosing perspective.

8.2 Seeing 2

This morning, while meditating, I thought about seeing; about how I see my life, how I see myself, how I see my children, my business, my day. The whole works. I decided to see my day as bountiful. I decided to see my life as safe; a place of safety and security. I decided to see my children as *right*, as okay, as complete, strong and whole. I decided to see my business as strong.

A voice really hit me. 'As I see, so it is.' As I see others, so I see myself. It's a formula. I'm not sure if it came to me as a question or a reality. A thought? A whimsy? A curiosity? A truth filtering in through me? It dawned on me. It has been dawning on me over time. It's been hitting me.

As I see, so I am? As I see, so I am. How I see myself creates how I am; the quality of my life. It's unbelievable, wonderful to realize that we have this choice, and this power. What an amazing gift to be given.

When I see myself as strong, secure, valuable, and courageous, then I experience myself as strong, secure, valued, and courageous. When I see myself as insecure, as unstable, then I am insecure and unstable.

It gets even bigger.

Let's play with this idea. The way that I see myself, has an impact on how I see others.

When I see myself as insecure, how does it impact how I see you?

I may see you as confident, content, secure, even though I have no idea how you actually feel. I may look for your faults as a way to feel better about myself. My seeing will impact my reacting. How I react to you. I may put you on a pedestal and act with too much deference. I may look to you for answers or have unrealistic expectations of you. I may keep my distance, shut down, not be myself, be afraid of what you will think of me. I may act larger than I am as a way to feel less intimidated—to be that person I think you want me to be—like you, confident and secure.

I am now reacting inauthentically. I am no longer genuine. The way I see myself has misguided how I react to you. Now my seeing impacts you. It will change how you are: How you are with me. You are reacting to an inauthentic me. You too have your own insecurities. Here's an example: I'm intimidated by you—something about you triggers my insecurities. Let's assume I go with my automatic distant reaction. My body is a little more rigid, my arms are crossed, I show less emotion in my voice and body language. You see me. You see the choreography of my distant reaction. Even though that's what you see, it's not what you interpret. You may interpret my *dance* as one of confidence. I have done this many times. I've interacted with folks who looked like they were confident. But I'd misinterpreted their *shut down* mode as confidence. Which just made me feel even less secure.

So here you are, interacting with me. Not the real me, but the *acting distant to protect myself from feeling insecure* me. You misread me and you transform into your version of feeling intimidated. Your counteraction may be to shut down too. Now we have a show down. Your shut down versus my shut down. Like two cowboys ready for a gun fight. How ridiculous. Two scared cowboys acting *tough* to counteract their own fears. The more you shut down the more I feel intimidated so I shut down more and now we are locked in a vicious cycle. How I see me impacts how you see me, which impacts how you see yourself, which impacts how I see you, which impacts how I see me, and so on and so on. This is going on every day in every interaction we have. All based on how I see myself and how you see yourself; that is where it starts.

Back to good enough. Do I see myself as good enough? This, *do I see myself as good enough* impacts everything. How I see myself. How I see you. How I think you see me. How I think God sees me. How I see God. How I see my life, your life, life in general.

There are many versions of this dance. You may get real chatty when feeling insecure, or maybe sarcastic, angry, or overly helpful. We each have our own versions, our own dances that we fall back on when the *feeling intimidated* music comes on. At the core, these versions all do the same thing—they protect ourselves from feeling insecure and afraid. They are a way to deal with thinking we are not good enough. How you are when I'm not even there? Because you too are looking at yourself through sight perspective. You are human. You too have your insecurities.

You have no real idea what is going on with me. I react to you out of insecurity, out of intimidation. I shut down, act defensive, hold back. You misread me. You read my shut down as confidence or a judgment of you. You see judgment. My insecurity is misread. Now you react. You may feel less than me. You go into your pattern of insecurity or intimidation. We are in a dance. A dance based on a misguided perspective. Your dance may result in shut down mode or arrogance mode. Either triggers a response in me, whether it's more shut down or more arrogance. And the dance keeps going. The dance keeps going on. It's a wonder we get anything done. We are reacting and counter-reacting to mirages of ourselves and others. All based on seeing. On how we see.

8.3 Seeing 3: Seeing with Light

Here's our way out. Here's the way out. One of us has to have the courage or the insight to be authentic. One of us has to have the courage to choose a new dance. A dance of authenticity. Of honestly sharing how we feel. Of letting our guard down and sharing who we truly are. Accepting the risk of rejection, we go for real. We choose to see ourselves with honor, with respect. "Mark, I'm scared." "Joe, did I ever tell you about our daughter who died?" "Lisa, I am so pissed off at my family" "Claire, I have been grieving for 10 years." This is our light. Our authenticity is our light. It's how we see each other clearly. In the light. A similar dance can occur, in the light. As I speak my light, you see me as I am, which gives you the ability to see yourself more clearly. Instead of intimidating each other, instead of dancing to mirages, we help each other be real, be genuine, be authentic. The dance changes to a dance of realness. We still feed off each other, but now we are feeding off our light. Light begetting more light. We strengthen each other's light. The planet literally becomes lighter. We become lighter. More real. More light. Stronger, more confident, more enduring. Kinder. Gentler. More powerful.

8.4 Seeing 4: Seeing My Day

How do I see my day? Do I see my day as a space of danger, of troubles; or do I see my day as bountiful, plentiful, and full of opportunity? As I see my day, so goes my day. Regardless of the actual events. I may still get a flat tire, either way. How I see my day. How far does it go? Can I create more green lights, more parking spaces, more wonderful business relationships if I see my day as free, open, and wonderful? This is a great thing to try out for ourselves. Do I see my day as alive, as a friend—as a friend who is loving and caring for me? Actually, actively caring for me. On my side, on our side. Do I see my day as spacious, full of time, with plenty of time? Can you imagine the impact this has on you, on me? It means I can take my time. Is my day a spring of faith, of hope, of wonderful opportunity?

Expand it beyond one day, or one month. How do I see my life, our lives? I have spent many years seeing my life as a test, as a scarce place; a dangerous, vindictive, unstable place where bad stuff is bound to happen. Imagine if we can change our life by how we see. I have started and continue to see life building. I see more of my life from a perspective of bounty, of security, of being loved. I'm living a life where I am loved, cared for, provided for. It is safe. Then I'm seeing myself as capable in this life, as brilliant. Full of brilliance, hope, courageous, a sculpture, smart, talented, capable, blessed. I'm seeing this. I'm choosing to see this.

8.5 Seeing 5: Big Ripples

It goes beyond us. Remember, the way I see myself impacts how I see you which impacts how you see yourself. But this goes way beyond just the two of us. It impacts your family. It changes how your family sees itself. It impacts communities. It impacts nations. It impacts historical eras. All of this is made up of people. Individuals. All seeing each other. That's why our work is so important. It isn't just about ourselves. We're not just breaking, freeing ourselves from our own addictions to struggle. As I see myself differently, I see myself in more light, it will impact how I see you and thus how you see yourself. Extrapolate and multiply this over and over again. Rippling out through families, communities, nations. Imagine the impact of more and more people seeing themselves and seeing one another in light. Big changes we're talking about here. Big ripples. Big impact. Can you imagine the power our collective seeing has? How each one of us sees is impacting ourselves, everyone we touch, life itself. Every one of us. And as the old saying goes—*it starts with me.* How you see yourself has a huge impact on you and on the bigger you—your family, your community, your nation, your historical era.

8.6 Seeing 6: Still Fear

Sometimes I'm still seeing from fear, from concern, from doubt. It takes work. It takes courage for me to change how I see; especially when I'm caught up in fear seeing. It takes something to let go of its stronghold. The fear seeing seems so real. So definite. It takes work, considerable work, to change how I see. To see with more faith. To see with more trust. To see light when I'm seeing in darkness. Imagine the impact of seeing through hope.

8.7 Seeing 7: More Choice

Again, it's a choice. The addiction to struggle tells us there is no choice. That's one of its great strategies. In this case, seeing robs us of our ability to choose how we see. There is no choice in seeing. We can't choose how we see. But as we arrive at enough, at love, then we get more choice. More choice to choose how we see. How I see this moment. This situation. How I see you. How I see myself. How we come to see ourselves, our families, communities, our time in history. As we continue down our roads to enoughness we get more and more choice. More choice in how we see. Can you imagine how powerful this is?

We get to choose how we see. We get to create how we live.

9

Thinking

9.1 Thinking

We are creating the texture of our lives. It isn't happening to us. I used to think I was some kind of voodoo doll—being pricked and prodded by the universe. My life was not my own but the byproduct of a mean-spirited, testy, unloving, creating force. The voodoo doll owner was doing this to me. I was unaware of my contribution, how my creative forces were actually behind this *voodoo doll pricking*. I was the creative agent. It is a true blessing to start to realize the extent to which we create our lives. It was scary as hell at first; still is sometimes. It sounds great—this idea that we take responsibility for our lives. But if you don't think you are good enough, then how could you take good care of yourself? If you see yourself as *not good enough*, then how can you be a very good shepherd? You might think that you can overcome your deficiencies and be a good shepherd for others, but if we truly are the creators of our lives and we are deficient, not good enough at our core, how the hell could we take proper care of ourselves and others? Would you want to turn your life over to a creator that just wasn't that good? No wonder we walk around tentative and scared. Even the big shots, the cocky ones, are coming from fear. They don't want us to know that they know they are scared. So go big, act strong, look tough. It's all a ruse.

When we start to feel, to see ourselves as good enough, then we are freed to start doing this creating thing in earnest. I'm not sure which comes first. It all probably happens simultaneously. As we start to see ourselves as more whole, we start to realize our creative possibility. It's easier to see ourselves as creating our own lives when we see ourselves as capable. It's easier to take responsibility when we see ourselves as *enough*. That just makes sense. As we start to embrace the idea that we are co-creating our lives, we start to see ourselves more wonderfully, wholly, confidently. It all feeds off ourselves.

But it doesn't start or stop with our seeing. Seeing is just one of our creative tools. Thinking, that has to be right up there too. As we think, what we think, how we think, these too are the seeds that we drop, the sculpting that we do to create the texture and quality of our lives. And as we saw with seeing, it goes beyond ourselves. Our thinking impacts our children, our spouses, our friends, our businesses, our families; everyone. As we think, so we are.

In the Bible, it says that God said, "Let there be light and there was light." It could read, 'think there is light and there will be light' or 'say it is light and there is light.' Very powerful.

It doesn't stop at thinking and seeing. Speaking. Our words, the words we speak, do this same creating thing for ourselves and for others. The way others see, think, and speak has an impact on us. They are helping to create the quality and texture of our lives.

And it doesn't stop there. Hearing comes into play too. How do we hear, what do we listen to, pay attention to, recognize? What do we choose to hear? You got it—it impacts us and others. It doesn't stop there. Breathing, touching, walking, writing, eating; all of it. You get it: all of it impacts who we are, how we experience our lives; the actual lives we are creating for ourselves and for others. We are creating the texture and quality of our lives. We are. It's a gift God had given us. It's only scary to the extent we see ourselves as *not good enough*. That's the only thing that makes it scary.

We are not alone. God loves us. He gives us plenty, bountiful, the source of angels, of forces working for our good, caring for us. Giving us a pallet of beauty and bounty to work with.

9.2 Complete Package

There is nothing missing, nothing lacking. We, ourselves, are whole and complete. We are perfect. We come with God with us. We are complete as we are. With our faults, with our fears, with our concerns, our joys, our dreams, our hopes. Each one of us. Can you see this? Can you speak this? Can you think this? If you can; you are. But even if you can't; you are. We each are. We are perfect creations of a perfect divine source. A complete package of love. A complete package of love. Nothing off, nothing wrong. Can you choose to see this; to think this?

9.3 Craving

In struggle, we crave tension.

We think that anxiety comes from procrastination, from worry, from unrealistic expectations. We think it comes from running late, being treated poorly by others, by too much work to do. We've got it backwards. We need tension. We seek anxiety, so we go about doing things that will bring it to us. We procrastinate because we want the anxiety. We run late because we want the tension. We set up unrealistic expectations because we want the feeling it produces. We are tension farmers. We are brilliant at it. We desire the crop. We plant the seeds, we nurture, fertilize, weed out the peacefulness, we harvest it. We eat it. We celebrate it. We honor others who reach it too.

We know why. Because we don't think we are good enough, we have to make up the difference. We have to fill in the gap of *enoughness*. We have to prove our worth. Tension, anxiety, worry, doubt, overwork—yeah, that will do it.

Now change it. Crave peace. Crave peace. Crave peace. Desire it, plant, nurture, fertilize, harvest, eat. Peace, Joy, Enrichment. Crave it.

Once we know that we are enough, then we can crave it. Become enough, find enough, find out that you are enough, that we are enough; that life is bountiful, full, loved, cared for. Know that God loves us, or a spirit, or higher power. Realize that you love yourself.

Now there is space, there is reason, there is an ability to crave peace. *Enough* gives us peace. *Not enough* gives us tension. Crave peace. Crave enough.

10

Assessing

10.1 Assessing 1: Misdirection

I got off the phone and started to criticize myself. It was difficult. They had changed the agreement. It caught me off guard. I was mad, frustrated; felt deceived. This has been going on for a long time. I started to judge how I handled it. I should have answered differently. I didn't say the right thing. I should have....

I am sure that you can relate to this phenomenon. Why do we do this? What is the benefit? How have we been taught, trained to do this? To criticize ourselves. There has to be some life-affirming impulse behind it. We don't just beat ourselves up for the sake of it. All of our hardness, judgement, and sabotaging behaviors are grounded in life. There is some part of us that believes that if we do this it will be good for us. There has to be.

Have you ever seen a plant purposefully try to grow into a weaker state? No. Life organisms are imbued with life. A loving, creative force creates us chock-full of divine power. We are alive. We are

174 | ADDICTED TO STRUGGLE

born alive. We are born to live (sorry, Bruce, not to run).

When we exhibit a life-draining habit or behavior, it's because we have somehow misguided our life missile. We have given it the wrong coordinates. We have directed it toward darkness and told it that it was light. Our purpose is always life-affirming. Our directions, our interpretation of what it means to live, gets off course, gets misaligned. We misinterpret, misdirect.

Let's analyze how we have misdirected our life force so that it thinks, believes, and follows a path toward more sabotaging or destructive behaviors. In this case, being hard on ourselves.

Let's look at the *good* that can come out it: I make this call. It doesn't go the way I want. I feel threatened. I feel undermined. I trusted an agreement and now this person is going back on the agreement. Now my hardness kicks in. What is it trying to accomplish? What is its objective?

To protect me. It has to be. Its purpose is to sustain life. It has detected an anti-life action. I have been hurt. It is here to protect me. Someone broke an agreement. They are not trustworthy. My life-affirming response is to be hard on myself. This sounds a bit crazy. What does that accomplish for me? I want to get mad. I want to attack this person. I want to defend myself. I want to get my money. I want the money. They have something I think I need. I sense that they have control over something that I want. They are in control of a resource that I think is necessary. I am angry. And I'm afraid. I'm afraid that we won't get what we need. The money. The sustenance. We need it. They don't know how close we are financially. How tight the situation feels. They don't know this. We think we really need it. And they are holding it back. I'm afraid. I'm afraid of something else. If I let them know our situation, then I'll be in even more trouble—and I'll appear more vulnerable. They will respect us less. We'll never get the money. We'll never get the work. I think that if they know what's really going on in our financial life, we will lose their trust in this professional manner. 'How could they be good at this if they are struggling financially?' I'm sure this is what they would think.

I'm angry too. I'm afraid of my anger. If they find out I'm angry, then, again, they'll hold back our money. They will lose respect for us. They'll think, 'How can we trust him to do this work if he's angry?' I think I'm in trouble. I need to control myself. I need to hold back. I can't let this anger out. I can't let them know our financial predicament. I can't let them know how I really feel.

None of this may be true. But it sure seems it to me. Somehow I have acquired this belief system. I have no sense that it may or may not be true. It is just real to me—my internal guidance system. My life-affirming system has detected this threat. It's being told this information. It's being fed these *truths*. It will now react, just like a tree reacts to its sense of where the light is. A tree will bend and contort to get to the light. We do the same. We're built this way. It's a very powerful strategy, but there's just one problem. Our light detection system is askew. What we think is light—in this case, the truth that I believe—may not be real light. I think it's light, so I contort to it. We react in such a way to sustain our life force. Plants and life forces do something else—they move away from the threat, the anti-life forces. They will contort themselves away from a threat just like they'll make their way to the light.

What if I do the same thing? In this case, I need to contort away from my fear, from my anger, from telling them our actual situation. *Not good enough* raises its head again. I'm not good enough to be myself. I need to hide me. And I have built-in quite a good system for doing this, for protecting myself: get hard on myself. Brilliant.

It's playing itself out right now. If you saw me last night—up in the middle of the night, worried, afraid, feeling vulnerable, barely holding it together. The feelings inside of me, the fearful thoughts, causing me to wake my wife up. 'Can we talk?' Needing to talk, needing her to hold me in bed, talk to me, soothe me. Would you still trust these words, this book, if you knew me? If you knew the scared, insecure, fearful thinking me? There's still a part of me that is afraid. Would you trust me if you saw me as I am? Again, not good enough. My fear stems from my own concern that I'm not good enough. So I'm looking to you for validation.

My self-judgement works perfectly; it's a great strategy. My mind immediately goes to me, what I did wrong. Which means I'm less than. I feel depleted. My thoughts are now focused on myself. Now I'm *safe*. As long as I'm doubting myself, my attention does not go to my anger, to my desire to confront this person, to defend myself, to take assertive action forward. My judgment keeps me complacent. Keeps me *safe*. It I get assertive and express my anger, if I call them on this lack of integrity, then I won't get what I want. What I think I need. The money. The resources. The food and sustenance that I think I need.

Can you see how this works? Can you watch the life force mechanism at work attempting to provide safety and security? It is working to protect me. The problem is not the life-saving attempt, it's the *offness* of my belief. It's not the mechanism, it's the direction I am giving it.

It and *I* have come to believe misinformation. Let's look at it.

> *I believe I need this resource from the client. Yes, we do need food and sustenance to live—which, in this case, is money.*
>
> *I believe that if I stand up for myself, then something bad will happen to me.*
>
> *I believe that if I express my anger, then that resource will be held back.*
>
> *I believe that the client is the authority in this case.*
>
> *I believe that the client is in control.*
>
> *I believe that my sustenance will come from them.*

With this set of beliefs intact, if I take assertive action, then I won't get what I need. The life force kicks in and creates a magnificent strategy to protect me and to provide me with what I need.

177 | ADDICTED TO STRUGGLE

The problem is not the mechanism. The problem is the direction. The belief system that I have developed. It may not be important to determine where it comes from. Clearly I have been taught this through parents, teachers, and the media. Essentially what we are being taught goes back to the essence of this book: We can't trust ourselves. We are not enough.

10.2 Assessing 2: Your Own Version

This is my version of the *Addicted to Struggle* story. Yours may take on a different theme. Maybe you have been taught to lash out, to yell, to scream, to get aggressive. Do you keep yourself busy a lot? Remember the purpose of our reactions: To protect ourselves. Your lashing out, yelling or keeping really busy is protecting you from something. That has to be its purpose. To protect you. To keep you alive.

Do you understand how this mechanism works for you? Your life guidance system is attempting to protect you and it's guiding you toward the light. It's protecting you because it detects danger. The thing you'd be doing if you *weren't so busy*. Caring for your newborn child? Standing up for yourself? Attempting to start a business? Your mechanism detects this as dangerous. To do that thing would be a threat. Don't do it, it's too dangerous. Your *too busy* is a great strategy. A great, life-sustaining mechanism. It wants you to grow toward the light. It believes that isolation is light; being a victim is light; staying in your comfort zone is light.

10.3 Protecting What?

Here's the harm: Rejection. What if you aren't a great parent? What if you stand up for yourself and lose the opportunity? What if you go after your goal and find out you just aren't good enough to succeed? At the beginning of this book we talked about a really big problem. The reason we don't want to look at ourselves. The really big problem is finding out that we actually aren't good enough. This is the big problem we are trying to avoid. It's just too big a risk to take. It's safer not to try. So we come up with a wonderful diversion strategy so that we don't have to take the big risk of finding out we aren't good enough. That is a real threat. If you are afraid you're not good enough, you won't try. It would be too devastating. Too scary to face. It's safer not to try.

Your strategy may be different. The key is to unlock the erroneous belief system that leads us to an erroneous living system. We are misguiding our guidance systems. We are misguiding our life-sustaining systems. We are winning a losing game. My God, how do we stop this? How do we start winning a winning game?

10.4 Assessing 3: Redirecting

If I trust myself—in this case, to express my anger or to stand up for myself—then to get assertive is to *die*, to cut myself off from the sustenance. We are taught not to trust ourselves. We are taught that we are not good enough.

If I do trust myself, if I believe that I am good enough, then this life force mechanism would take another tact. At the very least, even if I did nothing different on the call, I would get off the phone and those self-assessment voices would be supportive. They'd tell me that I did a good job. They would assess the situation as difficult. They would honor how well I handled a difficult situation. Good job, Evan, good job. They might even thank me. Thank me for being a good teammate. I did my job well for our organization, I did a good job of sustaining my own life organism. I did a good job.

If I trust myself, this assessment mechanism may make me aware of how I feel. The anger, the frustration, the feeling mistreated, the breaking of a trust. It will bring up these feelings. If I trusted myself, if I believed that I was good enough, then what would I do with these feelings? What would I do with my anger? My actual choices may not be the real issue, the key is that my choices and actions would emanate from a current source of enoughness.

That is the key.

Here are some possibilities.

Maybe I'd wait. I would breathe into the feeling. I would go deeper into it. I would look into my wisdom. I would let this feeling guide me; the wisdom within me. I'd let it guide me. I'd feel the feeling. I'd know that I wouldn't blow up by saying something stupid and ruining this thing. I'd know that it's not dangerous to be angry. I'd trust myself. I'd trust that I'd know what to do. I might be spontaneous and allow the words to flow out of me. To trust that the *right* words would come.

Or I could say nothing. I could wait, get off the phone and tell someone. I could call or talk to someone that I trust with my feelings, and trust that they know how to handle these feelings. I'd call someone who wouldn't inflame the feeling, or tell me to calm down. I'd call someone who loves me enough to listen. They'd listen. They'd ask me questions. They'd remind me that it's okay, normal to feel this way: That it's okay to feel frustrated, to feel afraid, to be concerned. That gives me relief. I'm not a loser for feeling this way. Not a loser that this happened. It's average. It's happened to them too. They've felt this way too.

Together we'd figure out a strategy for what to do—what to do with my feelings, what action to take. We'd talk about purpose. What is my purpose? What do we want to achieve? They'd build me up by sharing their experience; how they got through it. I'd feel better just talking to them. Knowing that I'm not alone. That I have nothing to feel ashamed about. I'd feel normal. This is average. They'd give me hope; a positive way to deal with this. They might remind me about how far I've come. They'd help me see the positive in the situation. We'd talk strategy—smart strategy about what to do.

I'd trust myself by talking to someone who trusts themselves. Who sees themselves as good enough. Who is on this road to progress. Someone I trust and who trusts me. Who believes in me. My trust in myself will build with their trust in me. I trust them. I have come to trust them. They will help me come to trust myself. To know that I'm good enough.

Then faith; my faith; kicks in. My God faith.

This person is not in control of my bounty or my sustenance. My real sustenance comes from God; the true source. The client can't stop it. If my money, my sustenance, doesn't come directly through them, it will come from another vehicle. They are not the source.

Now my higher purpose, my higher power, my higher form of knowledge kicks in. I'm not only good enough, I'm not alone either. I'm not alone. I'm not alone. I am sustained. I am cared for. My universe is not devoid. Life loves me. No one can hurt me; no one can hold back my good.

I can laugh now. I can laugh. I'm okay. I will be okay. I've always been okay. I always will be okay. These beliefs give me lift. I feel more alive. More safe. More free. I will be okay. Woo-hoo.

Now I can focus on action—what action to take. A much better, a much higher quality of action. I can now take action, good action, in confidence. I can focus on learning. What can I learn? What have I learned? What can I do differently next time? I can look at my progress. How far I have come. Look how far I have come.

Another step in *good enough*. Moving toward *good enough*. Letting go of struggle. Coming to know that I am loved. Coming to know that I'm good enough.

10.5 Assessing 4: Blessed Mechanism

We are blessed to have this assessment mechanism built in. It is an important life-sustaining, growing process—very important. It helps to keep us alive, protect us, help us grow, and achieve our fullest. It supports our dreams, our hopes, our highest purpose, our joy, our power, our fulfillment. It is always doing that. That is its purpose. It is a great soldier. Unrelenting, it will not deviate from its job. It is dedicated, loving to us. A great friend, comrade. Always on, never off, working to keep us alive. It is one of many of our life mechanisms. All have been created and tasked divinely: keep alive, stay alive, grow, and prosper. This is their purpose; it never deviates.

10.6 Assessing 5: Listening Well

It listens really well to our direction, to the belief systems we give it, to our choices. That is why our thinking, our habits, our beliefs, are so important. These mechanisms listen and take action. Can you see the problem here? It's not the mechanism, it's the direction we are giving it.

10.7 Assessing 6: Winning

As the book title says, we are winning a losing game. The mechanism always goes for the win. The issue is the *win* that we are defining. In this case, I have taught the mechanism that the *win* is to keep my mouth shut, stay complacent, don't stand up for myself. Because if I do, I will *lose*. It wants to win, it is designed to win. Winning means life-sustaining; growing. I have told it that to win means to keep my mouth shut. Don't confront, because that would mean loss. When I get off the phone and go into self-judgment, it keeps me quiet. So I win. The problem is that I have now won a losing game. I have won a game that stems from *not good enough*. I have won a game in the realm of *not good enough*. In the universe of *not good enough*, I have just played brilliantly. I have won!

10.8 Assessing 7: Sourcing

Can you see it? In the world of *good enough*, the assessment mechanism kicks in too. It has to. It has a job to do; but look at the difference it makes when it emanates from *good enough*. It is there to affirm and sustain our life organism. But look at the difference of the tack it takes. Look at the difference. I much prefer an outcome that lifts me up, that drives me to peace, to balance, to enthusiasm, joy and fulfillment; that teaches me endurance, and fortitude, the ability to persevere. To learn, to grow, to choose growth-affirming strategies, decisions that create more strength, more stability. That enhance relationships, build intimacy, build our capacity to be smart, to be loving, and caring individuals. Decisions that put us in tune with the positive flow of life, in consort with intuition, with divine knowledge, and timing—really good timing. That move me toward growth, towards my spiritual growth, to a closer, divine connection. To enough. To knowing that I am loved and cared for. To knowing that I am enough.

11

Hearing

11.1 Hearing 1

I feel anxiety, I feel fear. I have no idea that these feelings are re-lated to *not good enough*. I don't even hear it.

Sometimes I can hear the voice, most often it is running below the surface. When I can hear it, it talks to me in a voice I recognize— my voice. It's the voice who doesn't think I'm a very good son. Who says that I have not done enough. That I'm not doing enough. In certain moments I can hear this voice. It's there all along. I'm so used to it I don't even hear it. But it gnaws at me. I feel ashamed, less than. I look for validation from others. I feel a weakness be-cause I'm not enough. I feel the judgment. I take actions to over-come my *less-than-ness*. I do things that I don't want to. I act against my own inner voice because I don't trust it. I'm listening to the voice telling me that I'm not enough. This causes anxiety, doubt, insecurity, a lack of trust. I don't heed my own voice. I look to oth-ers to show me a model of how to act. Anger gets stirred up—the

inner anger that comes from not listening to and trusting myself.
It is painful. It impacts all kinds of decisions I make. It keeps me
from following my voice, my guidance system, my passion; because
I don't trust it. I'm diverted; trying to live another's life version
of me. I lose my sense of self all because I don't believe I'm good
enough. It is a terrible crime. A crime against ourselves. This is the
worst kind—more harmful than one perpetrated by another; more
harmful than a crime, than abuse of another. I'm amazed to see
how much of my pain and suffering comes from this belief that I'm
not good enough. What makes it worse is that I don't even realize
that it's going on.

11.2 Hearing 2: A New Voice

But there is a new voice starting to come through. Thank
God for this other voice. A voice of a friend who cares, who
knows—who really knows—who can tell us, witness for us, another truth. 'You are good enough.' This is such an important step
along the way. Clearly we need to progress to a point where we can
say, where we can witness for ourselves and believe in ourselves
that we are good enough. But we need a step, a step up, the help
and assistance, the vision, of another. One we trust who can tell us,
*You are good enough. You are a wonderful son. You have done enough.
You are doing enough. I love you. Yes, that is really what they are saying.
I love you. I believe in you. You are enough. You are enough.*

I am grateful to have people to talk to who believe in me, care
about me, and have experience in these matters. They know me
well, we have spoken many times. We've had very honest conversations about how I feel, how I think, how I am going through situations. They have gotten to know me and I them. So when I tell
them how I'm feeling, when I tell them about a situation I'm going
through with my parents, they tell me that I'm a good son. That
I have been a very good son. That I have done a lot for my folks.
Hearing this is pleasing to my ears. One of the greatest lines I have
ever heard anyone say was, 'we will love you until you learn to love

yourself.' The first time I heard this, the words shot right into my heart. I felt a deep sense of relief. I believed these words. They were some of the nicest, most soothing, comforting, relief-inducing, powerful words I have ever heard.

We will love you until you learn to love yourself.

We will love you until you learn to love yourself.

We will believe you are good enough until you realize for yourself, that yes, you are enough.

You are enough.

You are enough.

11.3 Hearing 3: Valuing

I hesitate to make a phone call to ask for something promised to me. Why am I afraid to make the call? Not because of what the guy will say, but that he will think that I'm asking for too much. That I'm being a pest. That is what my voices are telling me. But that isn't the real reason. The real reason I'm hesitant to pick up the phone is because I don't value myself enough. Why would he want to honor a promise to me? Why would he make this promise anyway? Not only am I not worth it, but also what I bring to the table isn't worth it. He promised to do this for me because I had done something for him. But I don't value my side of the equation. If I truly valued my side then it would be easy to call. He still may not honor his commitment but then it has nothing to do with me. If we traded $100 worth of services and I only thought mine was worth $20, then it will be hard to receive his services if I value them at more than $20. But if I truly value my side of the $100 then it would be easy to ask for his $100. I wouldn't be worried about his reaction if I valued myself, my contribution. It comes into play when we devalue ourselves. When our orientation system, our guidance system, is weakened by our own devaluing of our assets. We can blame our parents, or a boss, or society. They may have shared messages that don't value our gifts, our efforts, and our talent, but ultimately we are the ones walking around with the devalued attitude. We are making decisions, reacting to situations based on a devalued asset, us. We can't really wait for others to lift our value. It may happen from time to time. We feel appreciated, our spirits go up. We feel a surge of confidence. But the real answer is within ourselves. We need to realize our value. We need to realize our value. We need to increase our value in our own eyes. This is the most powerful value add we can have. We can even believe that God values us—that will give us a hit for a while—but eventually we need to find it in ourselves. Find, realize, honor our value, our voice, our perspective. We need to do this.

Love, self-love, is the key to getting out of the *not good enough* syndrome. This is the path, our path, the most valuable work we can do in life. Coming to realize our own value. Coming to value ourselves, coming to love ourselves. Coming to love ourselves.

11.4 Hearing 4: Backing Off

I am a good son, but my mind tells me that I am not doing enough for my father and my mother. What other nonsense do I tell myself that isn't true? If I tell myself that I am not doing enough on this project for my client. If I tell myself that I'm not good enough at managing money. If I tell myself that I'm not generous enough, or sensitive enough. If I tell myself that I don't work hard enough, or that I'm not smart enough. If I tell myself that I'm not a good enough father, if I tell myself that I don't spend enough time with my sons. If I tell myself this stuff, then what am I going to do? I will try harder, I will do more. I'll spend more time, do more stuff, work harder. But we already know that this won't work. The *more* won't fill the *less than*. We know how this addiction to struggle thing works already. Doing more won't fill the feeling of less. But something worse is about to happen—I will resent this voice. I will resent my attempt to do more. I will resent that the *more* won't fill the void. Part of me knows that I am doing enough; part of me knows that I'm playing a game that I'll never win. So I will do the next best thing. When I hear this voice of *not enough*, I resent it. So I will back off. I will stay away from my parents, I will back off from my children, I will start to resent my work, lose my creativity and enthusiasm. We back off. It's self-preservation—we back off, we disengage. We start living the lie of these voices. We become less of a child to our parents, less dedicated in our work, less involved with our children. We become distant. We become exactly what the lies in our head are telling us.

11.5 Hearing 5: Telling Them

Once we realize that the voices are a lie, then we begin the process of freedom. Remember, how we get out of this: one of the most effective ways is to tell someone. To tell someone who is not a deeply dedicated struggler, someone who is on the path of freedom and love, someone who truly loves us, cares for us, and wants us to succeed. Someone we trust. We tell them what is going on, we ask them for help.

I told Ralph about how I was feeling and the voices about not being a good enough son. He loves me, knows me and reconfirms—boldly—the truth that I am a very good son. He reminds me not to listen to any voice, mine or another's, who suggests in any way that I'm not a good enough son. I need to hear this. I need to take this in. I'm starting to come back to sanity. Maybe a question rings in my ears. What if I am a good enough son? Affirmations start to ring in my ears. 'I am a wonderful son; I am a caring and loving son.' We have discussed this already. I'm on the most important road, coming to believe it for myself. The Ralph's of the world are really important—their support is invaluable—but the bigger goal is for us to begin to believe for ourselves that we are good enough sons, good enough workers, good enough parents, good enough lovers, good enough. We know that we need to come to love ourselves. We know this already.

11.6 Hearing 6: Listening to Love

So what happens when we start to listen to new voices—voices of love and support? When I start to realize that this voice, the *I'm not a good enough son* one, is a lie, when I start to realize that it's a lie, then I can have a great a-ha. If this one's a lie, then probably the others are too. If my voices are telling me that I'm not working hard enough, then what if that too is a lie? What if I am a good worker? My voices—and remember, *my voices* are not just the ones in my head—are talking to me. *My voices* include all of my voices, all of the voices that impact me, that I listen to, that I allow to influence me. They could be the voices of friends, colleagues, parents, the news, or stuff that I read. You get it. All of these are voices that influence how we think about life and ourselves. Many of these voices, unwittingly, are building our case for *not good enough*. We should not blame them too much. I think you know why. Their voices are reflecting their own orientation, their own guidance system. They too are emanating from their voices that are telling them that they are *not good enough*. Even the bullying voices are coming from a *not good enough* perspective. Can you imagine a bully who isn't running on high octane *not good enough* fuel?

So what can happen when we start to realize, or to even consider, that all of these voices are a lie? What can happen when we start to listen to the voices who love us, who tell us we are good enough? What will happen if I start to tell myself that 'I'm a good enough son'? What would you do differently? If you started to believe that you were already doing enough as a worker, as a child, as a parent, lover, friend; what would you do differently?

At the very least, I can begin to let go of my struggle. When I'm listening to the *not good enough* voice, then either I need to do more, as in struggle, or I'll eventually start to do less. When I feel, believe, that I'm doing enough, then I don't have to do more. I can feel good about what I'm doing. I can feel a sense of relief, of calm, of joy. I can look at my accomplishments with gratitude. I can feel confident, proud—really proud. I can rest, I can stop, I can relax, I can take my time. I can start to live with more spaciousness. I don't have to fill up all my time with stuff to do. I can enjoy my time with my children more. I can start to drop my sense of obligatory time. I can start to enjoy my work. My resentments will start to go away. Here's the real kicker: I will feel freshened by my *enoughness*. Uplifted and confident. Once gratitude-filled, we start to feel appreciated, we feel good about our efforts and contributions. Rather than feeling tired, hard and resentful, we feel good about our contributions—so guess what we will do? We end up doing more good in these areas.

I can invest more positive energy, more joyous energy into the stuff I do. So I actually do become a better parent, a better son, a better lover. This is where there is room to play. My effort is no longer focused on filling a void, so my activity is generated from a place of love. Activity that comes from love is play, feels like play; is engaging, fun, with room to try new things, be creative, fun, intimate. Remember that play is intimate. When we let go of the struggle, our actions emanate from love and caring—this is called intimacy. We become more intimate with our friends, our parents, our children, ourselves. When we become more intimate, we become more playful. We love to play, we love the feeling of engagement, of impact, of joyous effort, and we naturally do more of higher quality. The struggle stuff is more too, but it's of lesser quality—it's rigid, obligatory, full of strife and effort, with much less love, freedom and creativity.

I can allow myself to feel excitement. 'This is great. I am doing great. This was great writing. I'm having a blast with my children. I really love my life.' Excitement. In struggle I need to work harder; in love, I can feel excitement.

Trust me, the people we care for will know the difference. They will feel the difference between obligatory, resentful action, and acts of love. They will know the difference. Their response will depend on their own level of *enoughness*. To the extent they are playing in the world of *enoughness* is the extent to which they can receive your love, your intimacy, your joy. You will feed off each other. Your level of *enoughness* and their level of *enoughness* will create some formula for collective *enoughness* which translates into the amount of intimacy and love you both can receive and generate. You can imagine how loving each other together can increase your *enoughness*. As I love you, as you receive my love, it starts to build my case for *enoughness*. Your love of me, your Ralph, is telling you that you are enough, which seeps into your voices, which builds your case for believing it yourself. Yes, you begin to love yourself more. You are doing the same for them. They start to become *more enough*. A cyclone: momentum, starts to build. As you both become more enough, you start to feed more and more off your *enoughness* and their *enoughness* which throws you both into more love, more intimacy, more play. Imagine this in a family or community: Building the equation of love, intimacy, play, *enoughness*. We can start to build an avalanche of this *enoughness*; of this love: Just like we have and do build avalanches of not *enoughness*, of struggle. Just like we have built a society, a culture, of struggle, we can build a society, a culture of love. Here's the best part: the lie of not enough drives us to do more. That's its message. But the real way we do more and more of the highest intellectually, emotionally and spiritually, is by realizing that we are enough, that we are loved. It's in this space that we actually will dedicate ourselves fully to doing our best work, our best parenting, our best society-fulfilling contributions. The struggle which tells us to do more leads to doing less and of less quality. It produces weaker results, aside from the poor feelings it generates. The *enough* orientation does the opposite—it produces our best results, personally, organizationally and societally, emotionally and spiritually. If we really care, then our best bet is to embrace our *enoughness*, to create more love, intimacy, and play. Our best bet is to drop the struggle.

When we start to realize this lie, when we again start to realize that we are enough, when we come from love of ourselves, then again we will respond quite differently. We can change our game. What would you do if someone rejected you? If you knew you were enough, what would you do?

Depending on their level of not *enoughness*, they may not be able to see it or realize it or value it. You understand this. On the surface they may even hate you for it. They can't handle the intimacy, the joy, the love. How could they? Being *not enough* means that we don't warrant, don't deserve, the greatest gifts there are: love, joy, attention. They will hate you for it. They will reject you, make fun of you, come at you harshly, condemn, criticize, and be distant. Our not *enoughness* will misunderstand their actions. When we are caught in the struggle, we will take their response to us and turn it on ourselves as evidence. Evidence that we are not enough, that we are *not good enough*. We will let it hurt our feelings. We will try harder, which will generate even more dislike from them, which will make us feel even more *less than*. We try harder, they reject, and a vicious cycle ensues. Eventually, we will back off and they will get what they want—no attention. They can't handle the intimacy, the love.

12

Talking

12.1 Talking or Praying

Louie—a.k.a. Who are you talking to?

We already discussed the importance to talking to *Ralph*. Those loving, supportive, out of the struggle friends, confidents, and playmates. My Ralph's include a Bob, a Tara, a Sharon, an Ali, and many more. There is also another one. I call him *Louie*. He has many other names too. Now remember the part about watching who we talk to, as in staying away from the in-the-struggle friends. See, their advice, their way of listening, is linked to a struggle path, so the outcome will take us further down the struggle staircase. Our struggle-loving friends will help move towards more struggle and less love.

Now get this: I call God, *Louie*, or I came to call God, *Louie*. It was at a time when I was starting to develop a new spiritual life, a new path in my spirituality. I wanted to talk to God, but the term *God* felt so heavy, so distant; the guy with the beard. The term God was linked to an image of God that I was raised with, that *my voices* had led me to, taught me about, this is the God that I had come to understand. At first I had no distinction between the God I had come to understand and God. They were one. I had no idea of other ideas about God. I'm sure I had other ideas, but they didn't seem valid. There was God. That was it. I wasn't even really aware of what I thought of this God, although the beliefs were firmly ingrained.

I came to think about this God because I was hearing messages about having faith in this God, of turning my will over to this God, of surrendering to this God. 'No way' was my reaction. As I started to think about it, I realized that I was pissed off at God. My life had gone to a deep level of struggle, for a long time. This God was fucked up. On one hand, why did this God allow this to happen? On another, why would God do this? As I started to talk about this, think about this, it was clear that God was punishing, vengeful, angry. He was one-sided; contractual. He was distant. He was a he, old, all into power, and raising power over us. A ruling God who made us do stuff if we wanted stuff. We had to pay him. I didn't trust him. Why would I want to surrender, to trust, to turn my will over to this guy? I don't even think he had my best interests in mind. Pain and suffering was his game. This sucked in my eyes.

In time, after talking to, and listening to, these no-struggle friends and guides, I slowly began to open my mind to another conception of God. A loving and caring God. An intimate and close God. It was a nice idea, but it seemed alien to me, foreign, Christian—from the other side. Raised as a Jew, I was worried that I would be a traitor if I went with the loving concept of God. The bigger issue here is that God too gets caught up in our struggle conversation. We can blame God for it. As if God created a struggle culture. But I think it's the other way around—everything gets caught up in our struggle culture, even our conception of God. It's not God's fault, it's ours. Our struggle mentality creates a distant, angry God, who lacks intimacy, warmth, and love. We are tested, on the test, trying to prove our worth to this God. Does this sound familiar? Do you see the pattern? Distant, lacking intimacy, having to prove ourselves, not enough as we are? This is the way we live in our own heads, how we relate to others, to our lives, to our work, and even to the God we have created. We have created a vengeful God—even our God supports the struggle world. See this is all about salvation: On the spiritual level and the human level. We are seeking *good enough*. We are seeking acceptance. We are seeking a passing grade at work, with our parents, with our lovers, children, friends, society, with ourselves, and with heaven. What we are really seeking is salvation. Acceptance into the heavens—the earthly ones and the heavenly ones. When I want acceptance from you as a friend, employee, or lover; what I am seeking is salvation. Full acceptance, full *okay-ness*, full *enoughness*. That is what salvation is. What I'm seeking from my life on earth is being good enough to get into the club, into the afterlife, into enoughness. Salvation is the ultimate enoughness.

Here is the irony. In struggle we create a God who is a struggle God. The one who will test us; punish us. Then we try to serve this God who will never really be satisfied. We are trying to satisfy an unsatisfiable God so that we can get his final approval—our salvation. But it won't work. How can you satisfy an unsatisfiable God? So our theology, our beliefs, set us up for more struggle. We need to struggle more so that we can get in. It's the only way. We've even concocted a God that supports our struggle. It's an amazingly deep conspiracy. Do you realize how deep this goes? How brilliant we are? We have become *addicted to struggle*. We need to fill it. That is what addicts want: more, more, more. A more that never satisfies and wants more. That's what it really wants—a deep sense of loneliness, pain, dissatisfaction, emptiness. A hunger that is never satisfied creates shame, pain, loss, hopelessness, death. The kind of death that grips you when you are alive. That is where this is going. So check out how brilliant and devious this struggle is. It goes to the God thing for more fuel. The God thing has so much fuel, energy, and dedication to it. The addiction needs fuel; it takes us to the most fuel-potent, dedicated source in our lives. It turns the God thing into a struggle thing. It lets our natural pursuit of divine get tricked into fueling the addiction. It creates a struggle God that we run after. It even uses God to get us.

The way out is the same as our way out on the earthly level. Who am I calling on the phone? When I shift my calls to the Ralph's of the world—the loving, caring supportive types—I start to develop love for myself. This is the real way out. The real way out is *Love*. The real way out is feeling loved—first by others, then by ourselves. We too can use the God force. Coming to believe that God loves us, coming to believe that we are divinely loved. This will go a LONG way to helping us love ourselves. A very long way. *Love* Fuel, Divine love fuel, is a very powerful force.

Who are we calling? Who are we calling? On the phone, in our quiet moments, when we are in pain, when we are in joy. Who are we calling? The same applies on the heavenly level. Who are we calling out to?

As God became too heavy for me, I needed a different kind of God. I started to adopt a God that was more loving, caring, supportive, friendly. God became less distant. God was becoming a buddy. Calling my buddy God seemed like calling my best friend *Sir* or *Mister*, or *Professor*, or *Boss*. All of the struggle, lacking-closeness, terms. God was too heavy for my buddy. I needed a better name. Our landlord, a cantankerous kind of guy, warmed up to us and became a lovingly kind—while still cantankerous—old dude. One day he tells me a story about a friend of his who called God Louie. I loved it: Louie. Now that was the kind of God I could talk to, hang out with, chat with, play with, tell my problems to, and rely on. *Louie*!

13

Approval

13.1 Playing it Safe

I play it safe too often. I play it safe to minimize feeling *not good enough* I hold back my enthusiasm. I hold back my best ideas; my passion. I'm hesitant to share it. What if you don't like it. What if you don't like me? What if you don't like my best stuff? That is what I'm really afraid of. My passion and enthusiasm is attached to the best of me, my best ideas; my joy. When I let them out I'm vulnerable. I'm not hiding. I'm giving you my best, my genuine self. If you reject that, then I'm really screwed. Because you just rejected the best I've got to offer. So I play it safe. My life comes out muted. My light held back a bit; on reserve. My fear is that I really am not good enough. The last thing I want to risk is finding that out for sure. So I hold myself back so not to risk finding out that I'm not good enough. It's an insurance policy. This way I have an out. I can justify your rejection. You didn't reject all of me, just a muted part of me. Safe. I keep it safe. Can you relate to this?

13.2 Need for Approval

My need for approval is part of the struggle phenomenon. It's an insatiable goal. I'm hoping that your approval of me will fill my need to feel good about myself. It's impossible to fulfill. We are bound to fail. It's perfect food for our struggle.

13.3 Thumbs Up

The way out is pretty clear: we won't get everyone's approval. Better yet, we don't need everyone's approval. There is actually only one person's approval we really need: Our own. Remember that when it comes to our confidants, our non-struggle buddies, our purpose is not to get their approval for the sake of it. They are not filling up our not good enough hole. Their real purpose is to help us approve of ourselves, to give ourselves the thumbs up, to help us know we are enough.

13.4 Heart

Heart is passion, excitement, joy. Great words. I love coming from my heart. For me it connotes love, being genuine, authenticity. Great stuff that feels good. It doesn't even have to be hard. When I'm in this mode, it's a joyous application of mind, body, and soul to an endeavor. An act of the heart; heartfelt. Not because I have to do this but because I want to. I enjoy it. I love you and want to do this for you. It's joyous. It's of the heart.

13.5 Soul

What does it mean to put my *soul* into it. That sounds like my giftedness. The gifts that I have been given in life: my intelligence, my intuition, my knowledge. My gifts of caring, of listening, of creativity. My ability to create new and vivacious ideas. It includes my timing and my ability to connect with great people. Some people call it my magic. They are amazed at the people I meet, who I connect with. Giftedness is my ease, my calm, my ability to create a safe atmosphere—one that is very authentic, fun, genuine. My gifts. Being nice to people, engendering niceness, caring about people, and loyalty. Not bad stuff. Bringing my soul to this for this client? Pretty good stuff. It's also the qualities that I have cultivated along with the stuff I was born with and taught. The best of me. The best of the people I know; the resources I have. It's unleashing all of it. Pretty good stuff for me and for my client. For me, I get to taste, experience, and play with this endeavor to gain the benefits, the resilience, the patience, and the persistence that comes with it. The sense of reward, of pride, of more learning, and inspiration. This comes for me and also for them. Our giftedness elicits others' giftedness, which may be different from ours. But we unleash each other's. I help them to unleash theirs. We feed off one another. Pretty good stuff.

13.6 Giftedness

Our giftedness feels easy. My friend Bob turned me onto this. Sometimes we don't respect our giftedness because it feels easy to us, it feels natural. We are so used to valuing struggle that we have to learn how to respect, honor, appreciate, trust, and seek ease. In one of my meditations that phrase hit me, 'my ease is *His* brilliance,' meaning that my ease, the experience of being in my brilliance, is God's divine brilliance. The reason it feels easier is because brilliance has been unleashed. Inspiration has been unleashed. The force that created the universe is unleashed. Not a bad ally for an executive retreat. This is the same brilliance that creates gravity and living cells that multiply. This is what I'm accessing with heart and soul. I have reason to be confident, to let go, to be excited, to trust. Heart and soul. Ease, brilliance, fulfillment.

13.7 Staking our Claim

Today, the 27th of July, I claim myself as a writer. A wonderful writer. A professional writer. A wordsmith with a powerful message. A valuable message. A true message. I am an inspired writer. I sit down to write. I have an idea in my head. A question.

A phrase. I sit down and write. Often I have no idea what I'm going to say. Often I think I need to know the whole thing ahead of time. Often I rehearse in my mind what to write. But, I sit down and write. I start and let the words, the ideas run through my fingers. Often I watch, I read, I hear these words. They are new ideas. Exciting ideas. I am the reader and I'm writing. Exciting to watch ideas come out, to form, to go in one direction. Let them go—will they come back? Will they ever make sense? But I know they will because I've watched them form, go out, and then come back. Wow, how cool is that? I love it. I love to write this way. A conduit, a vessel, I'm being played through. It is awesome. I have been writing this way since 1984 or so. That was almost 30 years ago. Today I claim myself as a writer. A real writer. An expert writer. A craftsman. A conduit for new and innovative ideas. No longer am I stupid, a hack, a bad writer, a fake. No longer can I live into the lies that my ideas are dumb, that I can't articulate them. That I'll look like a fool. No more. Today I am a writer. That last thing I ever thought I would be. A writer. Wow, a writer.

Staking our claim is a very powerful tool. It's something we can only do for ourselves. A million people can tell me I'm a great writer and it won't sink into my *enoughness* until I claim it. The cool thing is that we don't have to wait for some outside body to give us validation. We don't need a certificate from an external authority. We can choose to give it to ourselves. Actually it's the only way it works. We need to make a decision. Here's another cool thing. We don't have to wait until we feel it or believe it. We can claim it first. That's often how it works too. We have to claim it first for ourselves and eventually we'll come to believe it, to know it, to feel it. It's quite liberating. Think of all the stuff you can, I can, we can claim right now.

I'm a wonderful dad.

I'm a caring person.

I am lovely.

I have a lot to offer.

I like myself.

I like myself a lot.

I am an artist.

I am really good at my job.

I enjoy my work very much.

I am happy to be alive.

I love you.

I am wealthy.

I have plenty.

We are very healthy.

We are a happy family.

I like to fly.

I am whole.

I am complete.

I am wonderful just the way I am.

It is an awesome experience to claim our lives. And here is one last claim. We are the only ones who can claim it.

I am enough.

14

Prayer is Practical

14.1 As You, As I, As God

This morning I was reading a daily meditation and it suggested that I pray for others. It was a great piece—talking about how powerful prayer is in our lives: Real, impactful. It suggested that as we come to realize how powerful and impactful prayer has been in our own lives, that we start to pray for others. In my reading today, I was guided to pray affirmatively. To acknowledge the good, the perfection that already is. This is a wonderful way to pray. Instead of praying for something that doesn't already exist, instead we acknowledge and affirm that what we desire already does exist. We affirm its existence already.

I started to think of folks in my life. My mind went to people that I don't really like very much or that I see as needing something. The words *Strong, Powerful,* and *Right* came to me for the first person. To me they seem needy, wounded, and hard for me to deal with. Instead of these concepts, I thought, what if they are actually okay?

The words *Strong, Powerful,* and *Right* came to mind. With *right* I didn't mean that they are right and something else is wrong. I meant they were alright, okay, complete as they were. Not lacking, not less than, not off their mark, not missing their potential, or not enough in any way. They were okay; right. That was pretty cool. A much better way to see them. So I went onto another person that I'm not that fond of. Guess what words came to me?

Strong, Powerful, Right.

Okay, that felt great. So I went onto another and another. Same words. Then I went to people I love and guess what? The same words again. And again, and again.

Strong, Powerful, Right.

Wow, it seems that everyone I knew, I had judged as having some weakness and *not enoughness.* Judgement. I'm judging everyone as being off in some way. This was a clear one. Because there is another person that I see this way too: Me. Am I seeing the world through my own misjudgment of myself? Is my seeing myself as *not enough* affecting the way I see others? If I saw myself as *enough,* would I see them as *enough* too? Or, is it the other way around? Does the way I see others impact how I see myself; how I experience my own life? Maybe it doesn't matter which comes first. Clearly, they are aligned.

If I want to change the quality of my own life, if I want to change the quality of my relationships, if I would like to have a positive impact on others, then it seems that I can start to see them and myself differently.

Strong, Powerful, Right.

I can start to see myself this way, I can start to see others this way. I can start to see life itself this way. There is one other: God. I have been seeing God as *not enough.* What if I start to see God as *Enough.* Would that help me see myself as *enough?*

Me Enough,
You Enough,
God Enough.

14.2 Questions

My friend Gary has made many great suggestions to me. One day I was talking to him about some problem I was having. He suggested I pray on it—pray on it in some way I never had before. I thought that was a good suggestion. On my ride home I started by thinking of all the ways I do pray. I went through the list. Then I tried to think of something different. An idea hit me: Ask myself a question. Then keep asking myself questions. One after another without trying to answer them. Just keep asking questions. This was a neat idea. So I did it. It was like jazz, improvisational. One question led to another, and to another. I didn't edit or try to make them make logical sense, I just kept asking. At some point an idea popped into my mind. I don't recall what it was. But I knew that my prayer was answered. It was odd, fun, liberating, easy, and effective.

Questions are such a great tool. They liberate. They are a form of lubrication; by probing, getting us to think, opening new channels, new ideas. They suggest the possibility of hope, of something new, another way, a way out. Freedom. I still do this as a form of journaling—I start writing questions. It's lubricating, illuminating, new, frees me up, gets me unstuck. They are easy to do because you don't even have to answer them. How easy is that?

14.3 Sculpting

Last night I prayed for Tara. She was flying home from Minneapolis. There were lots of thunderstorms all evening. We affirmed a plane ride in a God cocoon. Calm, for the plane and for Tara. The thunder was going on and on. As I looked at the weather map, I saw a space between the thunder and lightning. I smiled, imagining her slipping through this space. Her ride was easy, right through. I could easily mark this off as the good judgment of the air traffic control folks. I'm sure they did play a part. But more and more I'm stopping to see this in another vein, to see the evidence of prayer as a very practical tool for driving and creating the fabric of our lives. It takes a bit of work to connect these dots. I want to see prayer. I was trained to see it as a nice thing to do, but not trained to see it as a sculpture, a chisel to the wood, as making real marks, as a true shaping tool of my life, as having real impact. I'm coming to see it differently. Real, with sculpting impact.

14.4 In

When I am afraid, I want to run away. I want to get out. I hold back, in reverse. There, but in reverse, spinning my wheels. I'm there but I want to get away. I want to run. I want to go somewhere else. I want to be alone. Away from everyone. I don't want you to see me. I think it is safe alone. I think it is safe to be alone, to get away, to run. I think it is safe. That is why I want to run. I am afraid. The safe place to be is alone. I tried this, in earnest. I did it really well. I lived like a hermit. I did not answer my phone for years. Really, for years. I would not answer my phone. I did not give out my phone number. I cut myself off from every friend, family member, anyone who knew me. I did it. I ran away. Once in a while, like once a year, my mother would leave me a message. She fucked it up. If only I could have had a whole year away, untouched by my folks. If I could get a year, then I would get better. I would be free. I would heal. I would find my true self. Untouched, unsoiled by the pressure I felt from you all. I could not find out who I was around you. I could not get away from your expectations, my assumptions, the ideas and patterns imbedded in me. The patterns that surfaced when I was around you. I had to get away. I did. It was painful—very painful. So I went further away. I thought that being away would do the trick. It did not work.

I still want to get away; be alone. I still think this is the answer—to get away. I still think it would work. I don't know if it ever has.

About 15 years ago I was leaving a therapist's office. I was feeling frustrated, really frustrated. It seemed that the same issue I had been dealing with for 15 years was still driving me. I couldn't believe it. As I was getting into my car, I spoke out in my frustration. Maybe despair. I'm not sure who I was talking to at the time, but I said out loud, "what am I going to do?" A clear voice spoke back to me. It was not my voice; it was a clear male voice within me. It was not a voice that I recognized. It said, 'Start telling the truth.' Tell the truth. How the hell was that going to help me with this issue? I wasn't so shocked that I clear voice was speaking to me, I was more surprised with the advice. It didn't add up. So I said back, "How is that going to help me with this?" And this dear, clear and strong voice repeated itself: 'Start telling the truth.' I wasn't sure what to do with this voice. What to do with, 'Start telling the truth.' The reason I had gone to see this therapist was because of a lie. I had lied and felt real shame about it. So I called my friend Lauren. I asked her to have dinner with me. She was one of the very few, if only, people that knew what was going on in my life. I'm not sure where this idea came from. It surely was a start in truth-telling. I was afraid that if I told her what I did, then she wouldn't be my friend anymore. At the time, it was one of the riskier things I had done in my life.

I had started this company. It was growing a bit and we had a big job in Florida. A lot was riding on this. Our client was using this job as a way to test us; to see if we could handle a much bigger job. I don't think we had ever done a job this big, and it was a program that we had never done before: *Boat building.* On the surface, the title of our work was team-building. Here was the idea: Get a group of people together and give them a dynamic exercise to do together. The concept was based on the idea that the same skills it would take to do this job would parallel the skills and dynamics at play in their real work. It's a pretty cool concept. By playing our *boat building game,* they could exercise their *how to work together better* muscles. We got this job to go to Florida and work with 150 people. 150 people building boats out of scraps of stuff. It was a new activity for us, the first time we were going to do it. We had a dozen people flying down to Florida to do an exercise we had never done, and it was a test for an even bigger job. A lot of pressure. But there was another piece of the puzzle that no one knew about. I was afraid to fly.

There was a lot that no one knew about me. I had been living in fear, with anxiety, for many years. In true isolation. I didn't talk to people about how I was feeling, what I was really going through. For the most part I tried to hide it. My greatest fear was to reveal it. The fear and shame that if people knew what I was going through, I would lose their respect, their friendship; that if they knew of me and my weaknesses, my vulnerabilities, they would reject me. It's a fear that many of us have. The whole time we planned this job, the biggest fear I had was what to do with my fear of flying. It was constantly running behind the scenes. As the day of the job loomed closer, my anxiety level increased. I couldn't get on the plane and I couldn't tell anyone about it. The night before was a very restless one. I didn't know what to do and went back and forth all night: Go or not go. Then it hit me—lie. Tell them that I was sick, really sick. That would be a valid excuse. It would get me off the hook without losing face. Who could hold that against me? I was sick. Early that morning I called the main person who worked for me and told her that I couldn't go because I was sick. If I felt better I would get a later flight—another lie. At first there was a sense of relief, but then the shame kicked in. I couldn't believe I had done it. It was this shame that drove me to go see a therapist that I had seen for years. She told me that it had to do with my relationship with my mother. I couldn't believe it. All these years of therapy spent talking about my relationship with my mother. Had I not made any progress? It was in this deep frustration that I called out to the skies, "What am I going to do?'

I sat down with Lauren. I was going to tell her what had happened.

I was sure that she wouldn't be my friend anymore. I was sure she'd say something like, "How the hell could you do something like that? How terrible… I can't be your friend anymore." Looking back, I can see this as ridiculous. What I had done just wasn't that bad, but at the time, having lived in such a cocoon, it seemed like a huge admission.

As we are eating I get up the courage—and that is exactly what it was for me—and I tell her. Instead of the rejection, something quite amazing happened. She gave me a hug. I don't recall her exact words, but what came back was love. Not rejection; love. It will go down as one of the most amazing and transformational moments of my life. One that has repeated itself many times. In the face of sure rejection, I get back love. In the face of rejection comes love. One of the most amazing realizations in my life that has been repeated many times. It's still amazing, the sense of relief that comes over me. Expecting rejection, I get love. Not just love, but respect, love, care. Expecting rejection, I receive respect, love, honor. You've got to be kidding me. [Still I ask, what the hell does this have to do with my mother?] Expecting rejection, trained to be rejected, I take the risk and I get love. I take the risk to be myself, to tell my truth. I've been trained to expect rejection, hardness, 'What's wrong with you?', but what I get back is the opposition— respect, closeness, warmth, love, trust. I tell them a truth and they trust me? I expect to not be trusted, to be seen as weak, untrustworthy, to not be respected and what I get back is love. You've got to be kidding me. The world changed forever for me. It's as if the laws of gravity were turned on their head. What, the world isn't flat? The earth is round? Are you kidding me? It was exhilarating. A huge pressure relief valve released. The world is not only round, it just became safer for me, much safer.

When I sat down to write this piece called *In*, my intention was to write about the dynamic of being *in*; as *in* the game, *involved*, part of, into it, being a part of and feeling a part of. Not on the side lines, not part *in* and part *out*, but committed to. About throwing yourself into something, about being committed. I know what it's like to sit on the fence, to be *in* but not fully *in*. I was leading a retreat. It was for a team of leaders. One company had bought another. The leadership team was a mix of the old and the new. Their leader wanted to have a retreat, to build camaraderie, to have fun together, and mostly to build trust. One of the best exercises we do is called *Artifact*. It's quite simple. Everyone is asked to bring an artifact, a thing from home that represents who they aspire to be. I love this exercise. It is a simple way to get people to open up, to open their hearts; and ours. We get to learn about who they really are, facts about their lives, about people who have inspired them, the things they love to do, their passions, events that have transformed their lives, the people who have touched them. If you asked someone to talk about their passions, their trials, their inspirations, their life philosophies, the critical junctures in their lives, it might be intimidating and risky. But when you get to hold a thing in your hand and tell a story, it becomes much easier. Through this artifact, a huge door into them opens up. For a group of people who rarely open up, this can be a great exercise. It always amazes me that people who have worked together for 15 years know so little about each other. They know details, but they often know little about what's in someone's heart, what inspires them, who they truly are. Being the isolator I was, this shouldn't be hard to figure out, but it still amazes me. One of the folks told an amazing story about his athletic career. His artifacts were his letter jackets from two universities. The first university was the school of his dreams—since he'd been 12 he wanted to go there. He told a great story about accompanying his cousin to the school. It was so beautiful. He just knew that was the place for him. He was a good enough runner to run there. The coach promised him a scholarship if he was able to accomplish certain goals. He did, but the coach reneged on his promise— twice. Not only did he feel mistreated, he couldn't afford the school and had to leave his dream place. A coach from another university was a fan. He offered him a scholarship. As he left the office he felt a great sense of relief. But something else happened. This is what

211 | ADDICTED TO STRUGGLE

really caught my attention. In that moment, something came over him. He decided he was going to do whatever it took for him to do his best, to fully realize his talent. While he had trained well at the other school, he hadn't given his all. He had done enough. In this moment something deeper happened. It wasn't just an intellectual decision; it came from a much deeper place. He would throw himself *in. Fully In.* Whatever he could do to do his best. He committed himself fully. *In. In. In.* He had made a decision, something was unleashed in him. He was in—100% *In.* It was powerful to listen to. It was a powerful story. When a decision like this happens to us, it's so much more than a thought to do one thing over another. This comes from the soul. It was a have-to, a deep want-to, a need to, a desire, an issuing forth, an inner demand. Not because someone else told him to do it but because he wanted to, needed to. You could hear and feel the freedom, the release into something. It was beautiful and inspiring.

I have spent much of my life on the fence. Doing stuff, usually out of obligation. Thinking I had to, because it was the right thing, because others needed me to, I needed to. This is very different from being *In*; the kind of *in* where you want to, need to for yourself, are compelled to, love to. This is not fulfilling an obligation of another, of an outer expiation—this comes from within. Unleashing what is inside us. What we truly want to do and need to do—*In!*

This is the *In* I started to write about and as my story unfolded, another form of *In* appeared. As in *IN-timacy.* As I started to tell the truth, revealing the parts of me that I wanted to hide or was ashamed of, something really special happened. I started to experience intimacy. Real genuine closeness with folks. This intimacy put me *In* relationship with people. It was a powerful way of being *In* life. The truth-telling helped me feel part of, connected to, safer, more alive. The isolation kept me away, out of, but truth-telling did the opposite: *In. In* life, *In* relationship, *In*-volved. It opened the door, allowed me to come into others' lives. But something even bigger happened—I opened the door and let people *In. In* my life, into me, into my world. This *In* thing takes risk, it puts us in a vulnerable place. In many ways that is why we stay out. We think it's safer there, less of a risk, less vulnerable. The truth I found out is that I was much less stable, and more vulnerable, more at risk physically mentally and spiritually, living out. Out from people and out from myself. The other person we let *In* is ourselves. We are entering our world, getting inside ourselves. When I tell the truth not only do I let you *In*, I'm letting me *In*. It's a funny dynamic. In letting myself *out*, I am letting you *in*. In letting myself *out*, I let myself into myself. The greatest intimacy we can have is with ourselves. Being *Into* ourselves. Not in a selfish way but in a state of awareness, aware of who we truly are. This starts an even bigger process as we go into ourselves. In opens the door to something very special. It opens the door to a process. A process of acceptance.

We are afraid to really go into ourselves because of this *not good enough* thing. We are deathly afraid to find out that we truly aren't good enough. That is why we won't look inside. It's too scary, the risk of finding out that we really aren't good enough. It's a risk we need to take. It's in this looking in, getting to know ourselves, that we can confront our own insecurities, the voices who have told us we aren't enough; our own voice. This is the hero's journey, dragon-slaying at its best. Going *In* to discover that we truly are *enough*. The process of going *In*, of finding the peace and serenity that is within us. It's not out there. It's not out there in their approval, in good grades, in the pats on the back. We'll never find it out there. We'll find it *In*. Our allies, friends and mentors along this path will love us until we learn to love ourselves. Their role is not to give us the good enough. It's to give us the courage, the belief that we can find it in ourselves. They aid us by helping us go In, helping us realize that it's safe to go In: To confirm and reaffirm while we are on the path. It's safe, you are okay, it's okay to go forward, okay to go *In*.

It's *In* that we will find the other source of our security. We will find our God, our higher power, our source. It's all *in*, it's all in there. This is the journey. To go *in*, to find our own power within, to find

our God within. *In.* The answer is *In*, not *out.*
In.

14.5 Choose Faith

My journey for the past 30 years has been one of faith. Pure faith: Knowing that all is well; that I am being cared for, taken care of. Faith that I can talk to God. I can ask God for help. That help is always there. This is the faith I have been looking for. Faith that I'm not alone. Faith that I am not alone. Faith that my prayers are answered. Faith that I can ask God for help. Faith that God will answer my prayers. Faith that God is caring for me. Faith that I am being loved. Faith that I am being loved and cared for, right now. Faith that I can talk to this care-giving force. I can talk directly to this care-giving force. To know that I am being cared for. Faith that I have a personal relationship with this care-giver. I call him God, *Louie,* Lord. Faith in God. Faith in Louie. Faith in The Lord. This is the faith I have been looking for. Without this faith I was scared. Really scared. Alone; scared and alone. I still feel scared and alone at times. I seek out faith. After 30 years, I seek faith. Today I made a decision. I made a decision to have faith, regardless of what my mind might tell me. Today I am making a choice; a decision to have faith. I have been waiting for faith to take over. To just be there. Like a force of her own. Like a plant that has grown, a light that has grown. She has and now, today, I think she has left a little darkness for me. As a friend, as a gift, she has left a bit for me so that I could choose. She gave me the gift of choice. A space left over so I could choose her. I can choose to have faith. I can know that in the end I chose faith. I made a conscious decision to choose faith. In the face of concern, fear or doubt, she is giving me the choice. I get to choose faith. I get to receive the gifts of making that choice, the confidence, the courage, the blessedness, the feeling good inside, of knowing that I got to choose her. She has given me an amazing gift. I got to choose her. Today, at this moment, I choose faith.

In the movies, this would be one last choice and then I would go about my life living in blissful faith. I'm not sure it will work this way. My guess is that I will get to make this choice over and over again. I'm sure, if I look back on my life, I've made this decision many times. We get to a point where we need to make that choice. This feels a bit bigger. I'll let you know what happens.

14.6 Choose Faith, Part II

Now I get to choose faith in me. I didn't realize that was the path I was on. I had learned about God. My need for faith in God. Now I've come to realize that I want to have faith in me. To trust me. To trust my essence—the essence of who I am. To have faith in my story. The story of my life. To have faith in me. To know that I am enough. With my failings, with my shortcomings, with my deficiencies, with my lackings: I was enough. I am enough. I can trust myself. I can trust me. Trust my journey. Trust the essence of my journey. Trust that I will ask God for help. Trust my story. Trust the twists and turns. Trust me. I'm not even sure what this means to trust myself. I don't believe that it means that I can trust myself to handle any situation. I can't. *On my own*, I don't believe that I'm enough. I'm come to believe that I need God's help, and your help, the help of others. I can't do it alone. So what does it mean to trust myself?

15

Easy Does It

15.1 Ease Can Take Us There

This is why it's important to seek ease. Not to avoid pain necessarily, because the pain is taken care of. It will come; trust me. It might be right around the corner. So if we get our share, our allotment of struggle, then why seek more? Then we have the opportunity to seek, trust, look for, and cultivate ease. Be it at the gym, making decisions around the house, how to load the dishwasher. Seek ease. Seek the most ease you can find. Go beyond seeking it. Trust it.

Trust it.

I used to be a runner—mostly in high school. I ran hard; was taught that running well meant wanting to throw up when I was finished. That's how you knew if you ran *hard enough*. This was the image planted in my mind. It did not leave room for running to be fun or enjoyable to me. It was an exercise in hardness. Even as an adult, when I would run, this image was in my mind. I was shooting for this kind of exercise. Hard—that's what counted. I would run for a bit then stop. Years would go by and I'd start again. I never kept with it.

But one day I had an idea. I wanted to run again but was resisting getting started because it was too hard. Then I had a thought: What was making it hard? Could I remove the *hard* from running? If I could remove the resistance, could I run again? So I thought of the elements that were creating my resistance. It was pretty easy to figure out: Take away the *hard*. My *hard* was being created by a few things. One, take away the need for running to be a painful or hard endeavor. I could do this two ways:

1. I would run only as long as I wanted to. I would stop before it felt hard—regardless of how short it was.

2. I would run as slow as I needed for it to be easy. No need to run fast or push myself. As slow as I wanted.

These were the two elements creating my resistance. Distance and Speed. So I removed them. I changed the criteria from hard to easy. I would run easy—I could do this by regulating my distance and speed, as well as my expectation of a good run. I was changing the criteria of success. So I went to the track with my new criteria. I started to run, committed to only going as far as I wanted regardless of how short that was. As slow as was easy, regardless of how slow that was. Ease was my guide. It was great. I ran about 100 yards. At the first sign in my body or mind that I was hitting any resistance, I stopped. No pushing through. I stopped. I literally ran 100 yards and stopped. It was slower than a jog. I stopped. I was done. I had completed my work out. Fully complete. I was done and I left. It was one of the great victories of my life. I laughed at myself. It felt a bit ridiculous. It felt a bit irreverent. Like I had just gotten away with something. I may have even looked around to see if I got caught. If anyone saw this silliness. I had done it. I was done. I'm telling you, it was a great victory. I'm sure I laughed to myself. I even resisted the inclination to now *walk a bit* to make the workout complete. Instead I left. I walked off the track and got in my car. In fun I probably told myself, 'wow, that was a hard work out, I feel exhausted.' I hope I said that—made some fun of it. It was a great moment.

I had accomplished my goal. I was a runner again. How easy could I make the start of something? That was the biggest breakthrough. How do we reduce the resistance to doing something? Wipe out the resistance. Get rid of it. If we can get rid of the resistance, we can do anything. We'll want to do it. If we can reduce, get rid of, the elements that create our resistance, we could do all kinds of stuff. We'd want to do it.

I kept going back to the track with my same mantra. I don't care how far or how slow I go, as long as I stop before or as soon as I feel any resistance. Let's see what happens. The assumption is that you won't go very far. If we don't push ourselves, we won't grow, get better, or continue. WRONG. Absolutely wrong. I took on this same approach with rock climbing. I wanted to do it. I saw other people climbing at a rock gym; way up high. I could never do that. I was afraid of heights and had very little upper body strength. I wasn't adventuresome like these folks. I didn't have the push, the ability, the guts to do it. Then I had an idea. I would try. I would climb, but only as high as I wanted to. See into that world; like running. There is an emphasis on pushing yourself in rock climbing. When you see someone climbing and they stop, the culture is to encourage them to push, to push through their fear. 'Go further, you can do it.' Well, I decided to take that element out of it. I was curious. What would happen if I didn't push myself? What would happen? Would I ever go any further? Would I only go a little bit? I wanted to challenge the notion that if we don't push ourselves, we'll never really progress. Could we progress with ease? With ease as our guide, would we progress? I wanted to challenge the 'no pain/no gain' mentality. See, I had evidence. I had evidence from my running. I had kept up my running game. Little by little, I started to want to run more. Without pushing myself, or having the goal, the need to run far or fast, I started to want to run more. My resistance, or desire to stop, naturally came later and later, I also started to run faster. It felt good. My approach of removing resistance led to me wanting to run. It was enjoyable, easy. I liked it. I naturally started to run further and faster. But I kept up with my philosophy. I didn't care how fast or slow, the goal was to remain easy, enjoyably. I saw the evidence of this approach. But would it work with climbing?

Again, I asked myself, what was my resistance? It was clear. Height. Height and ease. I would only climb as far as I felt comfortable. No push, only as far as I felt comfortable. Real success would be stopping even before I felt resistance, discomfort or fear. Stop short. Stop while I still felt comfortable. It felt a bit ridiculous—I would only climb 6 or 8 feet. In climbing you need a belayer, someone to hold your rope—you can't do it alone. I didn't know anyone who climbed there. So I had to ask someone to belay me. I felt a bit embarrassed—they would naturally encourage me to go higher. In hindsight, I should have been more transparent, told them my game. That would have reduced my discomfort. Instead I struggled a bit. I would resist their encouraging me to go higher, to push. In regards to struggle this is a fine example. My unwillingness to tell my truth, explain my game, actually created more struggle for me. It would have been a moment of discomfort to be honest about what I was doing. In order to avoid this discomfort and possible rejection, I chose a strategy that actually caused me more discomfort. I created my own struggle. If I would have just told them, then I could have more easily invested myself in my game. I may have even developed an ally who would encourage me to stop. I may have helped them with a new strategy.

Back to the story. I was committed to just going as high as I felt comfortable. So I did, wondering if I'd ever go higher. Six feet, eight feet, that was it, then I'd come down. Again, it felt a bit weird doing this, but I was committed to my experiment. So I kept this up, wondering what would happen. Six feet, eight feet, down. Easy, no strain, no fear. Easy.

Then something really cool happened. I got on the climb, prob-ably expecting another 8 foot climb, but it didn't happen. Very naturally and easily, boom, I climbed to the top—20 or 30 feet. Boom, all the way to the top. I jumped from 8 feet to 30. My ease zone; my ease expanded from 8 feet to 30 feet. It was awesome. A great climb. All the way to the top—more importantly, in ease, in comfort, enjoyable; no push. My *no push* had worked. It had worked, *ease* had worked. If there was any push involved at all, it was to my commitment. My commitment to ease. That was my real commitment. It had worked. I was flabbergasted. I had been taught '*no pain/no gain.*' This should not have worked in my pre-vailing philosophy. But it did. Brilliantly. I kept this up. Became a really good climber. Going beyond what I originally saw. The folks I watched—the ones I was sure I couldn't be like—I went beyond them. I became a really good climber. I loved it and got really strong as a climber. Loved it. Without the ease, I wouldn't have stayed with it. I definitely wouldn't have enjoyed it as much. I was sure that if I started from a perspective of pushing myself, then I'd always push myself. The pushing threshold would change, but I'd always be pushing some new boundary. I was amazed that this worked. Going with ease, with no push; I grew. I got better. I excelled. Amazing. Absolutely amazing. First with my running and now with climbing. Wow.

15.2 Brilliance: In Action, Over Time

It works. It really works. Try it. Sales calls, working out, eating better. Anything. It works. How can we take out our resistance? Where can we remove the hard? What if I don't push myself? The key is doing *It*. Finding a way to do *It*. Remove the resistance; the hard and do *It*. Start It. Keep doing *It*, whether it's writing a book, meditating; anything.

I wanted to start meditating again. I had heard of people sitting, for an hour. That seemed impossible. I couldn't sit still. I asked myself, how long could I sit easily? What would be a really easy amount of time to sit for? Literally, I decided on one minute. One minute. That was about all I could handle. I literally set an alarm for one minute. That may have felt long. Maybe I should have started with 10 seconds, but I started with a minute. I was dating a woman. She thought I was nuts when I asked her to let me know when one minute was up because I was meditating. But I did it. I felt a bit silly, but I did it. Eventually I too would meditate for an hour, even more sometimes. That was not my goal, though. Ease was. And it naturally led me to sitting for longer periods of time. I enjoyed it. It was easy.

We are so afraid of the ease. Too many voices tell us that hard is what counts. We confuse ease with lazy. Lazy is not taking action, not sticking with something, avoidance. Ease is about brilliance. About taking brilliant action. It's about a really smart strategy. It's about starting. Finding a brilliant way to start. Finding a brilliant way to keep something in action. To progress. That is *brilliance*. Starting and keeping it alive over time. It's about accomplishment, progress. engagement, growing. That is *brilliance* to me.

15.3 One Push Up

One push-up. You got it. One push-up. I wanted to start getting stronger again. Push-ups are a great exercise. But I always felt myself *pushing* to do a push-up. Feeling the resistance to do more. Maybe I could do 10, or 40, or 50. But the push would be there. Pushing myself to do as many as I could. I could *push* to 10 or 20. You know the feeling—the pushing, the heavy breathing, I hate that feeling. I really don't like it. So I resist starting. I know what I'm in for. You may ask, "What's the big deal? It only lasts a few seconds really. Then you feel better. What's the big deal?" Here's the big deal. We keep teaching our minds and bodies that the *push* is what we need to grow. We keep reinforcing the *no pain/no gain* philosophy. We keep feeding our need for struggle. We keep reminding ourselves that if there isn't strain then it isn't valuable; not worthwhile. We reinforce a very detrimental idea. That's why it's so important. It keeps a lie alive. It feeds it, proves it. We need to break out, remove, dismantle this lie. It is very pervasive. So what, just a few push-ups. But it's more—a lie, another moment of feeding a lie. It won't kill you, absolutely not. But here's a chance, again, to change your way of thinking. A chance to feed a new reality. Develop a new habit. A new way of being. A chance to feed, to fertilize a new reality. What an easy way to do it, with push-ups. An easy way to experiment, to develop, to plant another seed of ease. That's what this is about. Planting more and more seeds of ease. Building your own case. Proving for yourself that the strategy of ease works. Little by little, in safe and easy ways, disproving the myth of pain, of struggle.

So again, I asked myself, 'what would take away my struggle, my resistance in any situation? How do I use my brilliance?'

> *Do one push-up.*
>
> *Edit one sentence.*
>
> *Make one sales call.*
>
> *Clean one dish.*
>
> *Ask for help once.*

That's how I'd start. Do one push-up. How hard could that be? Take away the resistance.

> *Cultivate ease.*
>
> *Take action.*
>
> *Be Brilliant.*

16

Fun Wins Championships

16.1 What Makes It Fun For Me?

This is a great question to ask. It's part of the ease, a pathway to ease. Remember, *ease* equals your *brilliance*. Ease is your brilliance in action. Let's see how we can cultivate more ease, more brilliance. One way of doing this is by knowing what is fun for you. Just like a plant that grows well under certain conditions, we too thrive with ease and have fun under certain conditions. Not every plant does great in full sun, with very little water; in arid, dry, hot conditions. Cacti do. And some plants love shade, with lots of water; ferns love these conditions. It's one thing to want more joy, play, ease, fulfillment in our lives. It's a great goal. But do you know what does that for you? Do you know your own recipe for fun? What are the elements? It's not always apparent. Most of us are not readily aware of them. We may think we know, like taking a vacation. But not all vacations are fun and enjoyable. Maybe it's a day off, or some free time. But do you know what actually creates your fun for you? I stopped recently to take an inventory, to dissect, to come to understand what my fun elements are. I started by thinking of situations that I find enjoyable, peaceful, invigorating, fun. Then I played detective. What were the elements in each one? The next step is easy: Compare. What were the common elements? One for me is *choice*. When I feel or believe that I have choice in an endeavor, this gives me a much better chance of finding enjoyment, meaning, and fun. Am I choosing to write right now? Did I get to choose to go to the gym or does it feel *have to-ish*? Freedom to choose is a biggie. What's cool about this is that, even in a chore, a have to, I can take time and shift my perspective; see if I can find the choice in a *have-to* event. I'm so much better off when I can do this.

Tara and I give each other a night out each week. I often like to go to the gym. Recently I left around 4:00 and went to the gym. I had one of my *easy* workouts. I played with the machines and weights a bit, then hopped in the pool. I had a great swim. I just started swimming again. I had resisted swimming because each time I'd start, I'd get a pull deep in my leg, by my butt. Stretching wouldn't help, so I left it alone. But swimming always makes me, my body, feel so good. So I hopped in the pool again. My intention was ease. Finding a way to swim that wouldn't produce my strain. I played my *distance and speed don't matter* game. I started with some breast stroke. Did four or five nice, easy laps. Then went for a lap of freestyle. It's freestyle that creates the strain in my right leg. One of my swimmer friends told me he kicks very little—I did that. Then something cool, really cool, happened. I went back to the breast stroke because it was feeling easier. Freestyle was feeling harder. As I moved my arms, they started to swim out and about in a hugging-the-water movement. The movement was free, easy, big, and round. It felt really nice. I liked the resistance I felt in the water, the fullness, the pulling—like dough. It reminded me of some of the tai chi-like moves I like. And naturally my legs started to bend up toward my chest—fully, coming in contact with my chest and then, together pushing down and back. It felt great, like some new stroke. I kept it up. It felt very alive. I smiled. It dawned on me. Why am I limiting myself to the strokes I was taught? I'm not in some official race. I'm not in a swimming course, trying to perfect a stroke to get my next badge. There must be all kinds of strokes. If my purpose is not speed, or looking good, or passing some course, then—wow—I could make up all kinds of strokes. It felt great. My body was getting a great workout—my abs, arms, chest—it felt great, beautiful, free. I felt like I was playing, creating something new, something that worked for me. It also felt a little rebellious, breaking out of an authoritative *right* way of doing things. I love when that happens.

And I stopped.

I stopped while I was still in the ease stage. Then I moved through the water like a whale, jumping up, cruising back through the water, arcing through, coming up and jumping again. I love doing that, it's fun. I did it a lot as a kid and still do it with my kids. But usually not in the swimming lanes. That's the kind of thing you do in open water, playing with the kids, not as part of training, or exercising, in the swimming lanes. But I wasn't bothering anybody, nobody was around. It felt great. A wonderful way to finish. This too felt liberating. Breaking out of a *should*—as in how you should swim and finish in an adult swimming lane. I love this kind of beginning rebelliousness. A rebelliousness that is natural and authentic; without trying to be different or unique. One that is responding to an inner urge—to be unique, authentic, alive, experimenting in the moment. Finding something new. I got out, took a shower. I was in no rush. I got the shower to that perfect temperature. When you just want to stand under the water. The soothing water coming down on me at a perfect temperature. Perfect. I stayed there as long as I wanted to. Took my time, very relaxed, got dressed. Took my time.

As I got to my car, I felt done. I felt gently complete. Relaxed. And I knew what I wanted to do. I wanted to go home. It was only 5:30. I still had a lot of time on the clock of my free night out. There was some voice in my head—a voice telling me how I should use the rest of my time, that would be the right thing to do. I should go to a movie, go out to eat, go shopping, do something cool. Isn't that what I'm supposed to do? But I could feel it; I could hear it in my body. I was ready to go home. So I did. I was complete. What I wanted was to go home. That was the beauty of these free nights anyway: choice. Getting to choose what I wanted to do with my time. Not having an obligation at home—dinner, homework, doing stuff with children, cleaning. There were no obligations during free time. It was time to choose what I wanted to do. Freedom to tune into my own impulses, desires, intuitions, wants, needs, rhythms. Freedom in time. Freedom to choose. I chose to go home. Sometimes I choose to stay home. In those moments that's what I want to do with my free time. The children and Tara were surprised to see me come home—glad. I'm guessing she understood. I'm guessing she understood my choice. She knows me enough. I think she understood. Some part of her may have told me to stay out, it's okay to stay out, but I'm pretty sure she understood. I came home out of choice, not guilt or obligation, but out of choice. I got to come home and be with my family. I wanted to be with my family. Freedom of choice.

This is a great *fun* story for me. A classic Evan story. Let's go back, do some detective work and see what my fun elements are, what are included in my ingredients of meaningful. I like to write in books—you may not. If you are open to it, go back and circle the words and phrases that seem core to this story.

If you do this for yourself, you will find it to be a very rewarding and rich experience. It may be more fun and effective to do it with someone else, a playmate, to help each other discover your fun elements. Write your fun stories, then read through them—take your time—and catch the phrases and words that are your levers, the ones that make a difference, that put you in action, in your zone. Heck, you could spend a lifetime doing this. It's called getting to know yourself. It may be one of the core, most important ingredients in our spiritual lives: getting to really know ourselves, honestly.

This will be really rewarding for you as well as the people around you. Imagine once they get to know you better, what makes you tick, where your sweet spots are. That will make it much easier to get along with you, to work well with you, to care for you. They'll know what not to do too, what causes you struggle, deflates you, takes you out of your zone. This information is so important to ourselves and the people we are with—so important.

Here we go. I'll use my story as an example. Feel free to skip this section and work on your own. Dissect and be detectives of your own story.

The first clue I get is in the first few words: 'Tara and I.' This is all about agreement. We agreed to this through conversation, aware-ness. We had to talk, we had to come to this. We weren't following a script. We came to this. We agreed. We shared, without demand-ing. This is really important. I feel free from guilt, or at least have a lot less guilt. In agreement, we get support, support to go do. It also gives you practice in coming to agreements and building agree-ments with one another.

The second word that comes to me is 'care.' Our agreement is a way to care for one another, to care for ourselves. We came to this particular agreement so that we could take care of ourselves. We came to realize how important this free time was. Time to care for ourselves and one another.

We dedicated time to care. It is dedicated, planned out time. We can count on it. We don't have to wait to feeling overloaded. Doing so takes away crisis and creates security. It is dedicated time. We don't have to argue or fend for it. There is no demand of it because it is dedicated, secure, sure.

'Each week' means regular and recurring, enough. If it was once in a while or once a month, it might not be enough. Since it's each week and regular, I know it's coming. It even gives me freedom on other days of the week, knowing that this one is coming.

Its regularity gives me more freedom too, freedom to skip it. We don't always take it because it doesn't always make sense. We may have other obligations or stuff we want to do. We don't always need it. But knowing it's there once a week gives us great freedom.

We can't expect to have ease, fun, and peace in our lives when we are not attending to the stuff we need. Then it's just left up to chance. We get so much more control when we become aware of the stuff that makes it fun, alive, and secure for us.

We just finished the first sentence. You can see how rich this is. One sentence and look at the core stuff we've uncovered: freedom, regularity, dedication, care, agreement, awareness.

As we continue in this process, we become more masterful. Masterful bakers of our lives, of our peacefulness, meaningfulness, fun, joy, security. We become aware of our own ingredients, how to put them together and shape them. How to purposefully create the lives we want. To be able to bake the bread we want to be. Bread is substance and we are discovering how to direct our own substance, how to create the texture of our own lives. We can become more masterful. We will come to know our ingredients for peace and joy. We will know the bread that we want. We will learn how to make it; how to make ourselves. We gain so much more control over our lives, the texture of our lives. There is so much we don't have control over. This process gives us so much more control over the stuff few actually can control.

That is powerful. That is really powerful.

We can continue analyzing, breaking apart my story. We will find some ingredients that are really important to me, such as my creativity, having room to create new ways of doing things—especially ways that work for me, that are tuned in to my way of moving and being. I love doing that. It gives me great joy. I love creating new things, whether it's inventing a new kind of glove (I have, please ask me about my gloves when we meet), a new way to swim (I have, we can talk about this too), or discovering a style of writing that works for me (you are experiencing it). I love when I do this, when I can find my uniqueness and tend to it.

I love the feeling of being a little rebellious when it's authentic. Not because I'm trying to be rebellious or different but because my search for what works, what feels right, leads me to something new. Writing God on a tennis ball and playing tennis—it felt so wrong and yet so right. Now this was praying for me. When I first wore an earring because I saw Ben Vereen with one. I just loved it. It added a bit of joy because almost no guys on campus had one. I liked that too. Not to be different for the sake of being different but because my authentic genuine desire led me there. An added bonus. My new swim stroke was a perfect *find* for me. A great fulfilling of my rebelliousness. I think a lot of us are like this. Maybe all of us.

Being able to tune into and *feed* my own rhythms is a biggie for me. Listening to myself and knowing that I wanted to come home. Part of what makes this work for me is time. I had plenty of time. I was gone for 1.5 hours. But if I had had only 1.5 hours to work with, this scenario wouldn't have worked so well. Having plenty of time to play gave me the freedom to use the 1.5 hours. I wasn't on the clock. The 1.5 hours was the natural flow of *enough time* for me. I used this recently when I had an extra half hour between appointments. I stopped to ask myself what would be fun now. I had some extra time. I thought of stopping at a museum that I wanted to see. That would be fun for me. But I knew my ingredients. The half hour would not be enough to give me the freedom of movement. I would have been on the clock. Even though when I finally got to the museum I only stayed 20 minutes, I did it in a space of plenty of time. That was the natural amount of time I wanted to spend there. I was able to *feed* my natural rhythm. If I had gone to the museum when I only had 30 minutes, I would not have felt spaciousness, relaxed, and room to play. I would have had less of an ability to play with my time, to *feed* my rhythm. I only spent 20 minutes there but I needed the half hour space to give me freedom. Knowing my ingredients helped me make a choice, which is not to say that I wouldn't have enjoyed going that day, but this increased my chances. Instead I simply took my time driving home. I meandered a bit, went down a quiet street. I enjoyed my ride home because the extra 20 minutes gave me plenty of time to get where I was going. Plenty of time. That feeds my fun too, sensing that I have plenty of time. Again, this does not mean that I can't have fun with limited time, but I have a greater chance of the fun when I align with and *feed* my ingredients.

This is the big issue here. Knowing what gives us joy, meaning, security. Knowing ourselves, this is a big issue. As we know ourselves we can better create so much more ease in our lives. We don't have to fight up stream, to fight against ourselves, so much. Less struggle, better choices. We make better choices for ourselves. More *ease*, more peace; greater capacity to work through the difficult, painful times in our lives.

16.2 What is Fun?

When I think of the word *fun*, I have images of laughing, jumping up and down—big stuff like that. I almost don't want to use it in this book, in this section. I too succumb to seeing *fun* as being frivolous, not enough. I want to use words like *meaningful*, *secure*, and *joy*. But I hesitate to use the word *fun*.

Here's an option—a midway point between *no fun* and embracing *fun*. What if fun is a byproduct? A litmus test? When I am doing the things that give my life meaning, security, and joy; and the byproduct is fun. The fun experience can be a litmus test, a sign that I am on track, on my track. It's a sign. It lets me know that my ingredients are in play. A plant flowering; with the conditions right. Just like our cactus, or fern; we are blooming. Maybe *fun* is one way of blooming; knowing that we are in alignment with our ingredients. *Fun* is also fun. It feels good. I feel alive, at peace, tuned in when I'm having fun. Finding meaning, joy, camaraderie. It's a sign that I'm doing something I enjoy, in a way that I enjoy it, with folks I enjoy—even more evidence.

Fun may not be an ultimate life goal, but it can help. It can help guide more toward my sweet spot; toward the spot where I grow well. It is a valuable question to ask. A valuable question on our quest to know ourselves. It's a good tool. A guiding apparatus.

Fun is fun to have. Work gets done well when it's fun. *Fun* is engaging, uplifting, enjoyable. Fun is a good thing. Fun is a good part of life.

16.3 What Will Make this Easier?

Here's one of the key tools we've learned. We can always ask ourselves, 'what will make this easier?' This too is a great guide. What might make this easier? We can ask this about anything. Even when I'm in a lot of pain I can ask this of myself. What would make this easier—even if just a bit? The ease question, like the fun question, will guide us more to the light, toward a solution. Remember, *ease* equals *brilliance*. When we ask the ease question we are not trying to run away or avoid effort or responsibility. We are asking how to bring more brilliance, more peace, more room, more love, more fortitude, and more patience to the situation. For me it is often another person's help, asking God for help, prayer, meditation; all of them. Ease leads me out of despair, out of hopelessness. Ease will lead me to more faith, more hope, less struggle. A prayer might make this easier. Calling a friend, journaling, helping someone else, asking for help—each of these could make a painful situation easier. Changing my perspective, staying in the now—each of these can make it easier. Ease will help me with emotional pain, with a work situation, a messy home, a vacation— a choice of any kind. The core issue here is, again, letting go of struggle and leaning in toward a lighter way of being, a more brilliant, creative, effective way of being. That's where ease guides us.

What would change if I believed in the power, the rightness, and the validity of *ease*? Imagine what would happen to our work, money, relationships, child-rearing if we used *ease* to guide us. Can you imagine the impact on our health? Imagine if health was my natural state; robust, roaring, vital health? Really, what would change if we believed that?

16.4 It's Okay to Struggle

"Life is Hard." The first line in Scott Peck's *The Road Less Traveled*.

These three words touched me deeply the first time I read it. My life was hard at that time, harder than it had ever been. Scary hard. On top of the *hardness* was my judgement: 'I shouldn't be feeling this way. There is something wrong with me for feeling this way, this strongly, with my particular set of hard symptoms.'

It's funny, 30 years later, I'm going through it again. My father is very ill. He is in the process of dying. I am having a difficult time. A hard time with my own particular constellation of hard symptoms. Feelings, sensations, thoughts. It's lasting longer than I think it should. Judgement. Judging myself for how I am going through this.

So Scott Peck helped me that day and again today. "Life is hard." These three simple words let me know that it's okay. I'm okay. It's okay to go through tough times. There is nothing wrong or off with me. I'm not *not enough*.

The judgment increases the struggle.

It really is okay to struggle. Normal. Average. Be it financial problems, serious health issues, an ill parent, a child who is struggling, a flood in your home, or just the natural pain of living. This is all normal. We will all go through times of struggle, but our addiction to struggle increases it. It goes on top and fuels it deeper. It adds isolation and judgment to the pain we are already feeling. It stops us, inhibits us from seeking help, from using our tools, making a phone call, asking for help. Our addiction to struggle shows up in our thoughts. Telling us we are wrong, there is something wrong with us, we are not enough. It takes a difficult situation and makes it worse. It feeds off of the struggles we are experiencing and magnifies, eats, indulges them. Another way to increase our struggle. It is okay to struggle. Life is hard. We need not make it more so.

Play is not just for smiles; for the fun, easy-going times. Play can help us in our struggle. Play is a lubricant. Lubricants are great to use in tight situations. Struggle, hard times are tight, congested. They could use some play. What will give us some relief—bring some light into a dark situation, give us some freedom, some courage to move forward to try something new? These are great times—some of the best—to use play. To explore, discover, try something new. Give yourself a break. Change your perspective. Think in a way that will give you a drop more of peace. What will give you hope? Try something new. Try it on. Play with your pain, with your hardship. Try a new game. All the elements of play can come into play. It may mean doing one push up, or drying one dish when you feel like you can't do anything. Try one minor little prayer when you are afraid to pray. Write three words in a journal. Any little movement out of your stuck-ness. Try one little piece of hope. One little thought of faith, even just for ten seconds at a time if you need to. Play with your reactions. Try on a new one. Play will not automatically relieve your problem, but it will lubricate it. A little at a time. A little relief.

Over and over, a little adds up to a lot. *Play* at its finest, an amazing antidote to struggle.

17

My Friend Rick

I was nervous, heading up to NYC to lead a workshop on Change. I was feeling like a fraud. As I reviewed the program, it was clear to me that I needed to learn this stuff as much as anyone I would be teaching.

I shared this fear with my friend, Rick Ciurlino.

Rick responded with love, compassion, and caring. This is so critical for me to move out of struggle; the opportunity to share my fears and get love back, to be vulnerable and receive compassion. The world seems so much safer to me every time I experience this dynamic; receiving love when I expect rejection.

"Evan, we all teach what we need to learn. And, it's not an accident that you are going up there to teach them."

As soon as Rick shared this with me I felt free; my anxiety evaporated. My sense of being a fraud was gone. I realized it was ok that I needed to learn this material. I was the right person, as I am, to go teach it.

Being ok, as I am, especially in my vulnerability, relieves so much of the tension I feel. Knowing that I am 'right,' as I am, takes away much of my fear.

Rick's love unstruggled me. I realized I was ok.

This is a beautiful unstruggle pattern; one way to stop winning this losing game.

It goes like this:

Afraid of not being good enough, a.k.a. rejection, share our pain, get love back instead of the expected rejection, realize we are ok just the way we are; feel unleashed.

I've been hesitant to share this book because I need to learn this stuff as much as anyone. My head tells me, 'How can I release this book with confidence if I still need to learn it? I'm a fraud. If people knew how I really am; none of us can trust this information.'

Rick came to the rescue again; his voice is still in me. 'I am writing about what I need to learn; it is not an accident that I'm writing this.'

I'm coming to understand that being a good conveyer of ideas and being a student of those ideas can be the same thing.

Thank you for being on this journey with me. I trust we can help each other let go of our struggle and find more peace.

With love,

Evan

Index

Evan Marcus never set out to be addicted to struggle. None of us do, really.

Evan's spirituality has always been part of his life but it wasn't until his life started to fall apart in his early 20s that it became his purpose. Along his path, he has wandered through his roots in Judaism, over three years in a seminary, a Master's Degree in Somatic psychology, twenty years in a 12-step fellowship, and an ongoing study of broad and eclectic spiritual interests. Professionally, Evan and his wife Tara founded a leadership consulting organization, DillonMarcus. Their primary purpose is to help executive teams perform at a world-class level.

Evan has co-authored two previous books:
It's OK to Play and *Pheel the Love.*

NOTES

NOTES

NOTES

NOTES

NOTES

18641875R00154

Made in the USA
Middletown, DE
30 November 2018